THE
POINT
OF LAW

THE
Charities Acts

D1789464

MICHAEL KING

London: The Stationery Office

Applications for reproduction should be made in writing to The Stationery Office Limited, St Crispins, Duke Street, Norwich NR3 1PD.

The information contained in this publication is believed to be correct at the time of manufacture. Whilst care has been taken to ensure that the information is accurate, the publisher can accept no responsibility for any errors or ommissions or for changes to the details given. Every effort has been made to trace copyright holders and to obtain permission for the use of copyright material. The publishers will gladly receive any information enabling them to rectify any errors or omissions in subsequent editions.

Michael King has asserted his moral rights under the Copyright, Designs and Patents Act 1988, to be identified as the author of this work.

Crown copyright material reproduced with permission of Her Majesty's Stationery Office

A CIP catalogue record for this book is available from the British Library
A Library of Congress CIP catalogue record has been applied for

First published 2000

ISBN 0 11 702384 1

Printed in the United Kingdom for The Stationery Office by Albert Gait Ltd.
TN000316 C10 06/00 9385 12053

CONTENTS

THE CHARITIES ACT 1992   139

PART I CHARITIES   139

Charity property   139

PART II CONTROL OF FUND-RAISING FOR CHARITABLE INSTITUTIONS   143

Preliminary   144

Control of fund-raising   147

The Charities Acts 1992 and 1993

INTRODUCTION

Charity – a Creature of Case Law

There are two popular misconceptions about charities:-

First, that in order for a body to obtain charitable status, it needs to be registered with the Charity Commission.

Second, that the principles of charity law are all enshrined in the Charities Acts of 1992 and 1993.

What then is a charity and where are the principles of charity law to be found?

S.96(1) of the 1993 Act defines a charity as *"any institution, corporate or not, which is established for charitable purposes and is subject to the control of the High Court in the exercise of the Court's jurisdiction with respect to charities,"* while "charitable purposes" are defined by S.97(1) of that Act as *"purposes which are exclusively charitable according to the law of England and Wales"*. Those somewhat circular definitions do not help us to understand what a charity is, nor I think does Lord MacNaghten's observation in the 1891 Pemsel's Case[1] that the word charity *"unmistakably has a technical meaning in the strictest sense of the term, that is, a meaning clear and distinct peculiar to the law as understood and administered in this country ..."*.

In fact, in deciding what is charitable, the starting point for the Courts, even now, is the preamble to a statute of Elizabeth I, the Charitable Uses Act 1601, long since repealed, which sets out various types of charitable purpose, from the relief of the aged and the poor and the provision of education to the repair of churches and highways and the ransoming of prisoners.

The Courts have for centuries followed the spirit and intention of the 1601 statute and by analogy developed the law as to what purposes are charitable. In particular, Lord MacNaghten in Pemsel's Case[2] said that charity comprised four principal divisions, namely the relief of poverty, the advancement of education, the advancement of religion and other purposes beneficial to the community not falling under any of the preceding heads. This classification nowadays forms the basis of any consideration as to whether a particular institution's purpose is charitable. As we will see later, the Charity Commissioners for England and Wales do have an important role,

---

[1] Income Tax Special Purposes Commissioners v Pemsel [1891] AC531
[2] Income Tax Special Purposes Commissioners v Pemsel [1891] SC531

concurrently with the High Court, in adapting the concept of charity as society's needs change but they do not lightly depart from Court precedent.

A useful, practical guidance leaflet "Starting and Registering a Charity" is published by the Charity Commision (CC21).

At present there are approximately 187,000 registered charities in England and Wales but there are probably some 90,000 additional bodies which are charities but which do not have to register either because they do not meet the size limits for registration or because they are directly accountable to Parliament or to government bodies – see S.3 of the 1993 Act.

The 1992 Legislation

A report in 1987 by a committee chaired by Sir Philip Woodfield was quickly (in Whitehall terms) followed by a Government White Paper in 1989 and then by the Charities Act 1992 which in Part I introduced important new provisions to improve the supervision and monitoring of charities.

It was perhaps the publicity surrounding the 1992 Act that gave rise to the idea that the responsibilities of charity trustees stemmed from the Charities Act. In truth, the Act required trustees to follow re-defined procedures in order to demonstrate their public accountability and the Charity Commission took the opportunity to re-emphasise the responsibilities of charity trustees and the principles of charity law that had always been there.

The remainder of the 1992 Act was a response to public concern over fund-raising methods, dealt with under Part II of the 1992 Act, and public charitable collections (i.e. collections on the street and house to house) dealt with under Part III of the 1992 Act. As we shall see later, Part III has never been implemented.

The 1993 Legislation

The 1992 Act which was rushed through Parliament before the 1992 General Election, left several pieces of legislation affecting charities still in existence, albeit amended. The Charities Act 1993 consolidated three major pieces of charity legislation, the Charitable Trustees Incorporation Act 1872, the Charities Act 1960 and Part I of the 1992 Act.

Quite why this valuable consolidation did not include Parts II and III of the 1992 Act is unclear; most likely it was a combination of pressure on Parliamentary time and because Parts II and III effectively stand by themselves.

Deregulation

In response to the Conservative Government's "let's get rid of red tape" policy, there have been some minor amendments to the 1992 and 1993 legislation via the Deregulation and Contracting Out Act 1994 and these are incorporated in the Acts as you see printed in this book, as are the amendments brought about by other subsequent legislation.

Nomenclature

As already explained, much of the law and practice of charities has roots in the common law of England and Wales, in other words the law developed over hundreds of years by the Courts, rather than in twentieth century legislation. For this reason, some of the nomenclature used can be confusing and a brief explanation of some important words may help:

'Charitable Trust'

Technically a charitable trust arises when one or more people are given money or property to hold or distribute for charitable purposes; often these purposes will be set out in a Trust Deed, a Will or some other written constitution, but in theory the purposes of a charitable trust could be written on the back of an envelope or even not written down at all, but simply evidenced by the conduct of the donor and the people whom he has asked to carry out the charitable purposes.

'A Charity'

For the somewhat circular definition of a charity, see Section 96(1) and 97(1) of the 1993 Act, as mentioned above. However, a charity can be in one of several forms, usually with a particular type of governing document:

Form of Charity	Governing Document
• a charitable trust	Trust Deed or Charity Commission Scheme
• an unincorporated association	Constitution
• a company limited by guarantee	Memorandum and Articles of Association
• an industrial and provident Society	Rules approved by the Registrar of Friendly Societies
• a body established by Royal charter	Royal Charter
• a body established by statute	Act of Parliament

According to how a charity is established, it may constitutionally be subject to other statutory regulation such as the Trustee Act or the Companies Acts or may to a greater or lesser extent be subject to the Charities Acts.

'Trustee'

The definition of "charity trustee" is to be found in Section 97(1) of the 1993 Act and it means that whoever controls the management and administration of a charity is a charity trustee, even though that person may in practice be called trustee, governor, council member, company director, guardian or anything else.

'Cy-Près'

'Cy-*Près*' is an important legal concept, probably derived from Norman French and meaning "as close as possible". Under this concept, Courts have for centuries assumed the right to vary charitable trusts where these had failed or where it was illegal or impracticable to give effect to the donor's general charitable intentions. Judges had to decide what alternative objects would be as close as possible to those original charitable intentions. This concept has been expanded in S.13 of the 1993 Act.

The Charity Commission

The Charity Commissioners for England and Wales, known shortly as "the Charity Commission" is a department of the UK government responsible to the Courts for their decisions and to the Home Secretary for the way in which they use their resources. In this commentary they are referred simply to as "the Commission".

The Commission's stated aim is to promote public confidence in the integrity of charities so enabling them to play the central role they do in society. Although, as will be seen from this commentary, the Commission have substantial powers to investigate and to take corrective action when something has gone wrong in the management of a charity, the Commission has made strenuous efforts since the 1992 legislation to work with charities individually and with the charity sector collectively to guide charities towards best practice and to try to ensure that problems do not arise in the first place. In addition the Commission can, by means of Schemes or Orders, modernise the objects and administrative machinery of charities.

In 1999 70% of registered charities had an annual income of less than £10,000, while only the top 2% of registered charities – many of them household names – had an annual income of more than £1 million. It is therefore not surprising that the Commission's policy is to devote most of its resources to that 30% of registered charities which have an income of over £10,000 a year and which account for 98% of the £22.4 billion income received by registered charities.[3]

---

[3] Quarterly Facts and Figures for 1999 – Charity Commission Website

The Commission may make regulations, with the approval of Parliament, to charge fees for its services but currently regulations cover fees only for providing certain copy documents.

The Commission can be contacted in a number of ways.

General Enquiries
Telephone : 0870 333 0123
Minicom: 0870 333 0125
Website including the Register of Charities: http://www.charity-commission.gov.uk

The Commission's three offices are located as follows:

London	**Liverpool**	**Taunton**
Harmsworth House	2nd Floor	Woodfield House
13-15 Bouverie Street	20 Kings Parade	Tangier
London EC4Y 8DP	Queens Dock	Taunton TA1 4NL
Fax: 020 7674 2300	Liverpool L3 4DQ	Fax 01823 345003
	Fax: 0151 703 1555	

Trustee Benefit

It may be helpful for the reader of this commentary to understand that it is a long established rule of English law that a trustee cannot take a benefit from his trust unless the document governing the trust so allows. The Charity Commission are particularly assiduous in policing this "no-benefit rule" in relation to charity trustees and their stated view is that trustees "should work collectively .. and not allow private interests to influence them"[4] In other words a trustee must be careful not to allow his personal interests and those of the charity to conflict.

While many modern governing documents do allow a trustee to take a benefit on certain conditions, older governing documents generally say nothing about trustee benefit (in which case the no-benefit rule applies) or simply restate the rule of law, usually forbidding trustees to take any direct or indirect benefit.

Where the no-benefit rule has been breached, my experience is that the "errant trustees" have failed to understand that the no-benefit rule is not simply directed towards preventing trustees from stealing from their trust but is designed to prevent a trustee receiving any benefit, direct or indirect, unless that is allowed by the governing document.

These are examples of breaches of the no-benefit rule, even though made with the best of motives:-

- a trustee whose building company is paid for work carried out on the Charity's premises;

---

[4] "The Hallmarks of a Well-Run Charity" – Charity Commission CC60

- a surveyor who is a partner in a firm which charges professional fees to a Charity of which he is a trustee;

- a trustee who is appointed a non-executive director of his Charity's wholly-owned trading company and receives directors' fees.

- a trustee who is appointed Chief Executive of the Charity, even though he resigns as a trustee for that purpose.

- a trustee who is paid a small honorarium for preparing the accounts of the Charity, in order to recompense him for time off work.

In these and similar cases, the first duty of trustees is to ensure that the Charity is reimbursed with what it has paid out in breach of the no-benefit rule. The fact that the Charity may have got value for money or that the cost of the work carried out by a trustee was discounted has no direct bearing on this though the errant trustee may be able to ask the Court to relieve him from the duty to repay. Trustees who find themselves in this situation should obtain specialist professional advice immediately.

It is not however a breach of the no-benefit rule for trustees to receive reimbursement of out of pocket expenses, including travel, food and accommodation expenses, while on charity business.

Purpose of the Commentary

This commentary is intended to explain the Charities Acts 1992 and 1993 to the interested layman but it cannot be a definitive exposition of all the detailed law affecting charities and should not be relied upon in particular circumstances without taking appropriate professional advice.

Some of the statutory instruments or regulations made pursuant to the Charities Acts are mentioned in the commentary but none have been set out in detail in this book so in appropriate cases they will need to be separately considered and/or specialist legal advice obtained.

Because the 1993 Act consolidates previous legislation, including Part I of the 1992 Act, it is tackled first, followed by what remains of the 1992 Act.

Apart from some provisions which are identified in the commentary, the Charities Acts apply only to England and Wales. There is no body in Scotland equivalent to the Charity Commission and therefore no registration of charities there, but there is some supervision by the Lord Advocate and Court of Session of those bodies which are recognised by the Inland Revenue as being entitled to tax relief.

Acknowledgements and Further Reading

In addition to my family and friends in the law who have encouraged me to write this commentary, I would like to thank Stephen Slack and Ceinwen Thorne of the Charity Commission, Neil Bradley of the Home Office and Andrew Watt of the Institute of Charity Fundraising Managers for their ready help and assistance. Finally, very considerable thanks are due to my colleague Elizabeth Bowes-Smith for her ever-helpful comments and to my secretary Margaret Ramsey for her constant good humour in addition to her typing skills.

As already mentioned there is so much more to charity law than the Charities Acts of 1992 and 1993 and if the reader is interested in further exploration of the subject, I would suggest this additional reading to which I regularly turn:-

Elizabeth Cairns: *Charities: Law and Practice (3rd edition 1997)*

Charity Commission Website : http//www.charity-commission.gov.uk

Douglas Cracknell, Pesh Framjee, Adrian Longley and Francesca Quint: *Charities: The Law and Practice (1994 – looseleaf).*

Hubert Picarda QC: *The Law and Practice Relating to Charities (3rd edition 1999).*

O Tudor: *Law of Charities (8th edition 1995)*

Michael King,
Stone King, 13 Queen Square, Bath BA1 2HJ.

April 2000

Charities Act 1993

CHARITIES ACT 1993

In this part of the commentary reference to "the Act" is to the Charities Act 1993, references to section numbers are to sections of the Act. References to "the 1992 Act" are to the Charities Act 1992. Various other definitions are included in the Introduction.

An Act to consolidate the Charitable Trustees Incorporation Act 1872 and, except for certain spent or transitional provisions, the Charities Act 1960 and Part I of the Charities Act 1992

[27th May 1993]

BE IT ENACTED by the Queen's most Excellent Majesty, by and with the advice and consent of the Lords Spiritual and Temporal, and Commons, in this present Parliament assembled, and by the authority of the same, as follows:–

PART I

THE CHARITY COMMISSIONERS AND THE OFFICIAL CUSTODIAN FOR CHARITIES

1 The Charity Commissioners

(1) There shall continue to be a body of Charity Commissioners for England and Wales, and they shall have such functions as are conferred on them by this Act in addition to any functions under any other enactment for the time being in force.

(2) The provisions of Schedule 1 to this Act shall have effect with respect to the constitution and proceedings of the Commissioners and other matters relating to the Commissioners and their officers and employees.

(3) The Commissioners shall (without prejudice to their specific powers and duties under other enactments) have the general function of promoting the effective use of charitable resources by encouraging the development of better methods of administration, by giving charity trustees information or advice on any matter affecting the charity and by investigating and checking abuses.

(4) It shall be the general object of the Commissioners so to act in the case of any charity (unless it is a matter of altering its purposes) as best to promote and make effective the work of the charity in meeting the needs designated by its trusts; but the Commissioners shall not themselves have power to act in the administration of a charity.

(5) The Commissioners shall, as soon as possible after the end of every year, make to the Secretary of State a report on their operations during that year, and he shall lay a copy of the report before each House of Parliament.

> **S.1** – *Provides authority for the existence of the Commission and its work in supporting, informing and monitoring charities.*
>
> **S.1(3)** – *Gives the Commission authority to promote effective use of charitable resources by encouraging good practice as well as by investigating abuses.*
>
> **S.1(4)** – *Reaffirms that the Commission has a duty to promote the effectiveness of any particular charity but cannot run the charity itself; but see the powers under S.18 below.*

2 The official custodian for charities

(1) There shall continue to be an officer known as the official custodian for charities (in this Act referred to as "the official custodian") whose function it shall be to act as trustee for charities in the cases provided for by this Act; and the official custodian shall be by that name a corporation sole having perpetual succession and using an official seal which shall be officially and judicially noticed.

(2) Such officer of the Commissioners as they may from time to time designate shall be the official custodian.

(3) The official custodian shall perform his duties in accordance with such general or special directions as may be given him by the Commissioners, and his expenses (except those re-imbursed to him or recovered by him as trustee for any charity) shall be defrayed by the Commissioners.

(4) Anything which is required to or may be done by, to or before the official custodian may be done by, to or before any officer of the Commissioners generally or specially authorised by them to act for him during a vacancy in his office or otherwise.

(5) The official custodian shall not be liable as trustee for any charity in respect of any loss or of the mis-application of any property unless it is occasioned by or through the wilful neglect or default of the custodian or of any person acting for him; but the Consolidated Fund shall be liable to make good to a charity any sums for which the custodian may be liable by reason of any such neglect or default.

(6) The official custodian shall keep such books of account and such records in relation thereto as may be directed by the Treasury and shall prepare accounts in such form, in such manner and at such times as may be so directed.

(7) The accounts so prepared shall be examined and certified by the Comptroller and Auditor General, and the report to be made by the Commissioners to the Secretary of State for any year shall include a copy of the accounts so prepared for any period ending in or with the year and of the certificate and report of the Comptroller and Auditor General with respect to those accounts.

S.2 – *Provides authority for the existence of the Official Custodian for Charities who is an officer of the Commission. A custodian is a person or body which holds property for the trustees and must act on their lawful instructions. Following the 1992 legislation, the Official Custodian now only holds charity land and those investments and other property where the Commission has intervened to protect the assets of a charity.*

PART II
REGISTRATION AND NAMES OF CHARITIES

Registration of charities

3 The register of charities

(1) The Commissioners shall continue to keep a register of charities, which shall be kept by them in such manner as they think fit.

(2) There shall be entered in the register every charity not excepted by subsection (5) below; and a charity so excepted (other than one excepted by paragraph (a) of that subsection) may be entered in the register at the request of the charity, but (whether or not it was excepted at the time of registration) may at any time, and shall at the request of the charity, be removed from the register.

(3) The register shall contain—

(a) the name of every registered charity; and
(b) such other particulars of, and such other information relating to, every such charity as the Commissioners think fit.

(4) Any institution which no longer appears to the Commissioners to be a charity shall be removed from the register, with effect, where the removal is due to any change in its purposes or trusts, from the date of that change; and there shall also be removed from the register any charity which ceases to exist or does not operate.

(5) The following charities are not required to be registered—

(a) any charity comprised in Schedule 2 to this Act (in this Act referred to as an "exempt charity");
(b) any charity which is excepted by order or regulations;
(c) any charity which has neither—
(i) any permanent endowment, nor
(ii) the use or occupation of any land,

and whose income from all sources does not in aggregate amount to more than £1,000 a year;

and no charity is required to be registered in respect of any registered place of worship.

[(5A) In subsection (5) above, paragraph (a) shall be read as referring also to—

(a) any higher education corporation within the meaning of the Education Reform Act 1988, and

(b) any further education corporation within the meaning of the Further and Higher Education Act 1992]

[(5B) In addition, in subsection (5) above—

(a) paragraph (a) shall be read as referring also to—

(i) any body to which section 23(1)(a) or (b) of the School Standards and Framework Act 1998 applies, and

(ii) any Education Action Forum established by virtue of section 10(1) of that Act; and

(b) paragraph (b) shall be read as referring also to any foundation to which section 23(3) of that Act applies;

but an order of the Commissioners, or regulations made by the Secretary of State, may provide that section 23(3) of that Act shall cease to apply to any such foundation as is mentioned in that provision or to any such foundation of a description specified in the order or regulations.]

(6) With any application for a charity to be registered there shall be supplied to the Commissioners copies of its trusts (or, if they are not set out in any extant document, particulars of them), and such other documents or information as may be prescribed by regulations made by the Secretary of State or as the Commissioners may require for the purpose of the application.

(7) It shall be the duty—

(a) of the charity trustees of any charity which is not registered nor excepted from registration to apply for it to be registered, and to supply the documents and information required by subsection (6) above; and

(b) of the charity trustees (or last charity trustees) of any institution which is for the time being registered to notify the Commissioners if it ceases to exist, or if there is any change in its trusts or in the particulars of it entered in the register, and to supply to the Commissioners particulars of any such change and copies of any new trusts or alterations of the trusts.

(8) The register (including the entries cancelled when institutions are removed from the register) shall be open to public inspection at all reasonable times; and copies (or particulars) of the trusts of any registered charity as supplied to the Commissioners under this section shall, so long as it remains on the register, be kept by them and be open to public inspection at all reasonable times, except in so far as regulations made by the Secretary of State otherwise provide.

(9) Where any information contained in the register is not in documentary form, subsection (8) above shall be construed as requiring the information to be available for public inspection in legible form at all reasonable times.

(10) If the Commissioners so determine, subsection (8) above shall not apply to any particular information contained in the register and specified in their determination.

(11) Nothing in the foregoing subsections shall require any person to supply the Commissioners with copies of schemes for the administration of a charity made otherwise than by the court, or to notify the Commissioners of any change made with respect to a registered charity by such a scheme, or require a person, if he refers the Commissioners to a document or copy already in the possession of the Commissioners, to supply a further copy of the document; but where by virtue of this subsection a copy of any document need not be supplied to the Commissioners, a copy of it, if it relates to a registered charity, shall be open to inspection under subsection (8) above as if supplied to the Commissioners under this section.

(12) If the Secretary of State thinks it expedient to do so—

(a) in consequence of changes in the value of money, or
(b) with a view to extending the scope of the exception provided for by subsection (5)(c) above,

he may by order amend subsection (5)(c) by substituting a different sum for the sum for the time being specified there.

(13) The reference in subsection (5)(b) above to a charity which is excepted by order or regulations is to a charity which—

(a) is for the time being permanently or temporarily excepted by order of the Commissioners; or
(b) is of a description permanently or temporarily excepted by regulations made by the Secretary of State,

and which complies with any conditions of the exception.

(14) In this section "registered place of worship" means any land or building falling within section 9 of the Places of Worship Registration Act 1855 (that is to say, the land and buildings which if the Charities Act 1960 had not been passed, would by virtue of that section as amended by subsequent enactments be partially exempted from the operation of the Charitable Trusts Act 1853), and for the purposes of this subsection "building" includes part of a building.

S.3 – *Requires the Commission to maintain a register of charities which is open to the public. The register contains basic information for trustees, donors, beneficiaries, local authorities and voluntary bodies as well as for the Inland Revenue. Organisations which no longer exist or operate may be removed. The register can be accessed directly via the Internet - see the Introduction. Charities do not achieve charitable status as a result of registering with the Commission; on the contrary they have to register with the Commission as a consequence of being charities* unless *they are:*

- small – *a charity with an income below £1000 p.a. with no permanent endowment and no use or occupation of land.*

- a place of worship, *if registered under the Places of Worship Registration Act 1855.*

- exempt – *a list of exempt charities is contained in Schedule 2 of the Act. Most universities, further and higher education colleges, foundation and voluntary aided schools and certain national museums are exempt from registration. They are generally exempt because they are regulated by other arms of government; however they can still take advantage of the Commission's enabling powers, for example to make constitutional amendments.*

- excepted, *by an order of the Commission or by regulations, for example certain church and armed forces funds and certain funds held by boy scout or girl guide associations.*

While excepted and small charities do not have to register and need not submit annual reports and accounts to the Commission, they are nevertheless subject to the Commission's investigatory and monitoring powers.

S.3(6) – *Provides that on application for registration, charities must produce various documents. Currently the Commissioners require:*

- *the governing document, (e.g. Trust Deed, Memorandum and Articles of Association or Constitution)*

- *DEC1 – a form of consent by the trustees to accepting their role.*

- *APP1 – an application designed to monitor what the trustees intend to do and what benefits (if any) they will personally receive.*

- *other documents issued by the charity or its promotors (e.g. newsletters, press reports, videos, business plans). The Commission are looking ever more closely at the proposed activities of the body applying for registration to make sure that it has been established for exclusively charitable purposes.*

S.3(7) – *Imposes a positive duty on trustees to apply for registration if their charity is registerable and to supply information about any change in the trusts of their charity.*

S.3(8) – *Requires the Commission to keep the register open for public inspection, though what they make available is in their discretion.*

S.3(9) – *Allows information to be in computer form.*

S.3(11) – *Obviates the need for someone to supply further documents if he knows the Commissioners already have them.*

4 Effect of, and claims and objections to, registration

(1) An institution shall for all purposes other than rectification of the register be conclusively presumed to be or to have been a charity at any time when it is or was on the register of charities.

(2) Any person who is or may be affected by the registration of an institution as a charity may, on the ground that it is not a charity, object to its being entered by the Commissioners in the register, or apply to them for it to be removed from the register; and provision may be made by regulations made by the Secretary of State as to the manner in which any such objection or application is to be made, prosecuted or dealt with.

(3) An appeal against any decision of the Commissioners to enter or not to enter an institution in the register of charities, or to remove or not to remove an institution from the register, may be brought in the High Court by the Attorney General, or by the persons who are or claim to be the charity trustees of the institution, or by any person whose objection or application under subsection (2) above is disallowed by the decision.

(4) If there is an appeal to the High Court against any decision of the Commissioners to enter an institution in the register, or not to remove an institution from the register, then until the Commissioners are satisfied whether the decision of the Commissioners is or is not to stand, the entry in the register shall be maintained, but shall be in suspense and marked to indicate that it is in suspense; and for the purposes of subsection (1) above an institution shall be deemed not to be on the register during any period when the entry relating to it is in suspense under this subsection.

(5) Any question affecting the registration or removal from the register of an institution may, notwithstanding that it has been determined by a decision on appeal under subsection (3) above, be considered afresh by the Commissioners and shall not be concluded by that decision, if it appears to the Commissioners that there has been a change of circumstances or that the decision is inconsistent with a later judicial decision, whether given on such an appeal or not.

S.4(1) – *Although registration under S.3 does not give the institution charitable status, it is conclusively presumed to be charitable once on the register, which is important when seeking tax reliefs and repayments and for public recognition.*

S.4(2) – *Provides that anyone affected by registration can question the right of an institution to be registered. In practice this is limited to the Inland Revenue and rating authorities who naturally have a keen interest as to whether a particular organisation is or is not established for charitable purposes.*

S.4(3) *Allows appeals for or against a decision of the Commission on registration (including removal from the register) to be taken in the Chancery Division of the High Court. Pending the decision of the Court any registration would be in suspense. A decision on appeal under S.4(3) can be reconsidered by the Commission on new evidence or following new judicial precedent.*

5 Status of registered charity (other than small charity) to appear on official publications etc

(1) This section applies to a registered charity if its gross income in its last financial year exceeded [£10,000].

(2) Where this section applies to a registered charity, the fact that it is a registered charity shall be stated . . . in legible characters—

    (a) in all notices, advertisements and other documents issued by or on behalf of the charity and soliciting money or other property for the benefit of the charity;

    (b) in all bills of exchange, promissory notes, endorsements, cheques and orders for money or goods purporting to be signed on behalf of the charity; and

    (c) in all bills rendered by it and in all its invoices, receipts and letters of credit.

[(2A) The statement required by subsection (2) above shall be in English, except that, in the case of a document which is otherwise wholly in Welsh, the statement may be in Welsh if it consists of or includes the words "elusen cofrestredig" (the Welsh equivalent of "registered charity").]

(3) Subsection (2)(a) above has effect whether the solicitation is express or implied, and whether the money or other property is to be given for any consideration or not.

(4) If, in the case of a registered charity to which this section applies, any person issues or authorises the issue of any document falling within paragraph (a) or (c) of subsection (2) above [which does not contain the statement] required by that subsection, he shall be guilty of an offence and liable on summary conviction to a fine not exceeding level 3 on the standard scale.

(5) If, in the case of any such registered charity, any person signs any document falling within paragraph (b) of subsection (2) above [which does not contain the statement] required by that subsection, he shall be guilty of an offence and liable on summary conviction to a fine not exceeding level 3 on the standard scale.

(6) The Secretary of State may by order amend subsection (1) above by substituting a different sum for the sum for the time being specified there.

S.5 – *Part of the improved public accountability introduced in the 1992 Act was the requirement (backed by the sanction of a criminal offence) to include a registered charity's status on the documents which it produces, including invoices, advertisements and cheques. Since 1995 this does not apply to charities with an annual income of less than £10,000, though it is good practice to do so.*

The reference to charitable status must usually be in English, but if a document is written wholly in Welsh, the equivalent Welsh words may be used.

Technically there is no requirement to include the status on a charity's letterhead (unless it is an invoice or is asking for money) but it is good practice to do so and many charities also include the registration number, e.g. "the X Charity - Charity Registration No. 123456" *or* "the X Charity – a registered charity".

Charity names

6 Power of Commissioners to require charity's name to be changed

(1) Where this subsection applies to a charity, the Commissioners may give a direction requiring the name of the charity to be changed, within such period as is specified in the direction, to such other name as the charity trustees may determine with the approval of the Commissioners.

(2) Subsection (1) above applies to a charity if—

    (a) it is a registered charity and its name ("the registered name")—
        (i) is the same as, or
        (ii) is in the opinion of the Commissioners too like,

the name, at the time when the registered name was entered in the register in respect of the charity, of any other charity (whether registered or not);

    (b) the name of the charity is in the opinion of the Commissioners likely to mislead the public as to the true nature—
        (i) of the purposes of the charity as set out in its trusts, or
        (ii) of the activities which the charity carries on under its trusts in pursuit of those purposes;

(c) the name of the charity includes any word or expression for the time being specified in regulations made by the Secretary of State and the inclusion in its name of that word or expression is in the opinion of the Commissioners likely to mislead the public in any respect as to the status of the charity;

(d) the name of the charity is in the opinion of the Commissioners likely to give the impression that the charity is connected in some way with Her Majesty's Government or any local authority, or with any other body of persons or any individual, when it is not so connected; or

(e) the name of the charity is in the opinion of the Commissioners offensive;

and in this subsection any reference to the name of a charity is, in relation to a registered charity, a reference to the name by which it is registered.

(3) Any direction given by virtue of subsection (2)(a) above must be given within twelve months of the time when the registered name was entered in the register in respect of the charity.

(4) Any direction given under this section with respect to a charity shall be given to the charity trustees; and on receiving any such direction the charity trustees shall give effect to it notwithstanding anything in the trusts of the charity.

(5) Where the name of any charity is changed under this section, then (without prejudice to section 3(7)(b) above) it shall be the duty of the charity trustees forthwith to notify the Commissioners of the charity's new name and of the date on which the change occurred.

(6) A change of name by a charity under this section does not affect any rights or obligations of the charity; and any legal proceedings that might have been continued or commenced by or against it in its former name may be continued or commenced by or against it in its new name.

(7) Section 26(3) of the Companies Act 1985 (minor variations in names to be disregarded) shall apply for the purposes of this section as if the reference to section 26(1)(c) of that Act were a reference to subsection (2)(a) above.

(8) Any reference in this section to the charity trustees of a charity shall, in relation to a charity which is a company, be read as a reference to the directors of the company.

(9) Nothing in this section applies to an exempt charity.

> **S.6** – *Allows the Commission to direct a change of name if too similar to that of another charity or likely to mislead. Words such as 'Royal', 'National', 'Authority', 'Church' are carefully scrutinised - see the Charities (Misleading Names) Regulations 1992 (SI.1901). The section does not apply to an exempt charity.*

Charitable companies can also be required to change a name by the Registrar of Companies, though usually that would be on incorporation and therefore precede registration as a charity. The Registrar of Companies now requires written consent of the Commision before allowing incorporation of a company with "charity" or "charitable" in the name.

7 Effect of direction under s 6 where charity is a company

(1) Where any direction is given under section 6 above with respect to a charity which is a company, the direction shall be taken to require the name of the charity to be changed by resolution of the directors of the company.

(2) Section 380 of the Companies Act 1985 (registration etc of resolutions and agreements) shall apply to any resolution passed by the directors in compliance with any such direction.

(3) Where the name of such a charity is changed in compliance with any such direction, the registrar of companies—

(a) shall, subject to section 26 of the Companies Act 1985 (prohibition on registration of certain names), enter the new name on the register of companies in place of the former name, and

(b) shall issue a certificate of incorporation altered to meet the circumstances of the case;

and the change of name has effect from the date on which the altered certificate is issued.

S.7 – *Gives effect to a S.6 direction in respect of a charitable company, ensuring that the Registrar of Companies alters the name in accordance with the direction.*

PART III
COMMISSIONERS' INFORMATION POWERS

8 General power to institute inquiries

(1) The Commissioners may from time to time institute inquiries with regard to charities or a particular charity or class of charities, either generally or for particular purposes, but no such inquiry shall extend to any exempt charity.

(2) The Commissioners may either conduct such an inquiry themselves or appoint a person to conduct it and make a report to them.

(3) For the purposes of any such inquiry the Commissioners, or a person appointed by them to conduct it, may direct any person (subject to the provisions of this section)—

(a) to furnish accounts and statements in writing with respect to any matter in question at the inquiry, being a matter on which he has or can reasonably obtain information, or to return answers in writing to any questions or inquiries addressed to him on any such matter, and to verify any such accounts, statements or answers by statutory declaration;

(b) to furnish copies of documents in his custody or under his control which relate to any matter in question at the inquiry, and to verify any such copies by statutory declaration;

(c) to attend at a specified time and place and give evidence or produce any such documents.

(4) For the purposes of any such inquiry evidence may be taken on oath, and the person conducting the inquiry may for that purpose administer oaths, or may instead of administering an oath require the person examined to make and subscribe a declaration of the truth of the matters about which he is examined.

(5) The Commissioners may pay to any person the necessary expenses of his attendance to give evidence or produce documents for the purpose of an inquiry under this section, and a person shall not be required in obedience to a direction under paragraph (c) of subsection (3) above to go more than ten miles from his place of residence unless those expenses are paid or tendered to him.

(6) Where an inquiry has been held under this section, the Commissioners may either—

(a) cause the report of the person conducting the inquiry, or such other statement of the results of the inquiry as they think fit, to be printed and published, or

(b) publish any such report or statement in some other way which is calculated in their opinion to bring it to the attention of persons who may wish to make representations to them about the action to be taken.

(7) The council of a county or district, the Common Council of the City of London and the council of a London borough may contribute to the expenses of the Commissioners in connection with inquiries under this section into local charities in the council's area.

> **S.8** – *Although the Commission's stated objective is to help trustees of charities to function effectively and although they will try to resolve disputes and problems where there is no obvious fraud or malpractice, they are not slow to use their power to institute a "S.8 Inquiry" where, following evaluation, they believe that this is the only way to resolve a dispute or correct a problem which the trustees either do not see or are incapable of correcting.*

Under S.8(1) an Inquiry can be instituted in respect of an individual charity or certain groups of charities but the Commission has no power to investigate exempt charities (see S.3 and Schedule 2).

Although under S.8(2) the Commissioners can appoint anyone to carry out a S.8 Inquiry, in practice inquiries are carried out by the Commission's officers from the Investigation Division at one of their offices in London, Liverpool or Taunton.

Under S.8(3) a person can be required to produce documents or attend to give evidence, (which under S.8(4) may be taken on oath).

S.8(6) – *Allows the Commission to publish reports following S.8 Inquiries but they generally do so by way of advisory summaries in their annual reports and guidance leaflets. In appropriate cases they will name the charity investigated.*

9 Power to call for documents and search records

(1) The Commissioners may by order—

- (a) require any person to furnish them with any information in his possession which relates to any charity and is relevant to the discharge of their functions or of the functions of the official custodian;
- (b) require any person who has in his custody or under his control any document which relates to any charity and is relevant to the discharge of their functions or of the functions of the official custodian—
  - (i) to furnish them with a copy of or extract from the document, or
  - (ii) (unless the document forms part of the records or other documents of a court or of a public or local authority) to transmit the document itself to them for their inspection.

(2) Any officer of the Commissioners, if so authorised by them, shall be entitled without payment to inspect and take copies of or extracts from the records or other documents of any court, or of any public registry or office of records, for any purpose connected with the discharge of the functions of the Commissioners or of the official custodian.

(3) The Commissioners shall be entitled without payment to keep any copy or extract furnished to them under subsection (1) above; and where a document transmitted to them under that subsection for their inspection relates only to one or more charities and is not held by any person entitled as trustee or otherwise to the custody of it, the Commissioners may keep it or may deliver it to the charity trustees or to any other person who may be so entitled.

(4) No person properly having the custody of documents relating only to an exempt charity shall be required under subsection (1) above to transmit to the Commissioners any of those documents, or to furnish any copy of or extract from any of them.

(5) The rights conferred by subsection (2) above shall, in relation to information recorded otherwise than in legible form, include the right to require the information to be made available in legible form for inspection or for a copy or extract to be made of or from it.

> **S.9** – *The Commission has power to call for any documentary or other information and to search records – this is enforceable as for a High Court Order so that refusal can be contempt of court – see S.88.*

10 Disclosure of information to and by Commissioners

(1) Subject to subsection (2) below and to any express restriction imposed by or under any other enactment, a body or person to whom this section applies may disclose to the Charity Commissioners any information received by that body or person under or for the purposes of any enactment, where the disclosure is made by the body or person for the purpose of enabling or assisting the Commissioners to discharge any of their functions.

(2) Subsection (1) above shall not have effect in relation to the Commissioners of Customs and Excise or the Commissioners of Inland Revenue; but either of those bodies of Commissioners ("the relevant body") may disclose to the Charity Commissioners the following information—

(a) the name and address of any institution which has for any purpose been treated by the relevant body as established for charitable purposes;

(b) information as to the purposes of an institution and the trusts under which it is established or regulated, where the disclosure is made by the relevant body in order to give or obtain assistance in determining whether the institution ought for any purpose to be treated as established for charitable purposes; and

(c) information with respect to an institution which has for any purpose been treated as so established but which appears to the relevant body—
   (i) to be, or to have been, carrying on activities which are not charitable, or
   (ii) to be, or to have been, applying any of its funds for purposes which are not charitable.

(3) In subsection (2) above, any reference to an institution shall, in relation to the Commissioners of Inland Revenue, be construed as a reference to an institution in England and Wales.

(4) Subject to subsection (5) below, the Charity Commissioners may disclose to a body or person to whom this section applies any information received by them under or for the purposes of any enactment, where the disclosure is made by the Commissioners—

(a) for any purpose connected with the discharge of their functions, and

(b) for the purpose of enabling or assisting that body or person to discharge any of its or his functions.

(5) Where any information disclosed to the Charity Commissioners under subsection (1) or (2) above is so disclosed subject to any express restriction on the disclosure of the information by the Commissioners, the Commissioners' power of disclosure under subsection (4) above shall, in relation to the information, be exercisable by them subject to any such restriction.

(6) This section applies to the following bodies and persons—

(a) any government department (including a Northern Ireland department);

(b) any local authority;

(c) any constable; and

(d) any other body or person discharging functions of a public nature (including a body or person discharging regulatory functions in relation to any description of activities).

(7) In subsection (6)(d) above the reference to any such body or person as is there mentioned shall, in relation to a disclosure by the Charity Commissioners under subsection (4) above, be construed as including a reference to any such body or person in a country or territory outside the United Kingdom.

(8) Nothing in this section shall be construed as affecting any power of disclosure exercisable apart from this section.

(9) In this section "enactment" includes an enactment comprised in subordinate legislation (within the meaning of the Interpretation Act 1978).

S.10 – *Provides for mutual disclosure of information between the Commission and government departments (for example the Inland Revenue, the Police, the Department of Trade and Industry and the Home Office) to enable the Commission to carry out their functions.*

11 Supply of false or misleading information to Commissioners, etc

(1) Any person who knowingly or recklessly provides the Commissioners with information which is false or misleading in a material particular shall be guilty of an offence if the information—

(a) is provided in purported compliance with a requirement imposed by or under this Act; or

(b) is provided otherwise than as mentioned in paragraph (a) above but in circumstances in which the person providing the information intends, or could reasonably be expected to know, that it would be used by the Commissioners for the purpose of discharging their functions under this Act.

(2) Any person who wilfully alters, suppresses, conceals or destroys any document which he is or is liable to be required, by or under this Act, to produce to the Commissioners shall be guilty of an offence.

(3) Any person guilty of an offence under this section shall be liable—

(a) on summary conviction, to a fine not exceeding the statutory maximum;

(b) on conviction on indictment, to imprisonment for a term not exceeding two years or to a fine, or both.

(4) In this section references to the Commissioners include references to any person conducting an inquiry under section 8 above.

S.11 – *Creates a criminal offence of knowingly or recklessly providing false or misleading information to the Commission; this includes deliberate destruction of a document. It is often referred to in the course of S.8 Inquiries*

S.12 – *Repealed by Schedule 16 Data Protection Act 1998.*

PART IV
APPLICATION OF PROPERTY CY-PRÈS AND ASSISTANCE AND SUPERVISION OF CHARITIES BY COURT AND COMMISSIONERS

Extended powers of court and variation of charters

13 Occasions for applying property cy-près

(1) Subject to subsection (2) below, the circumstances in which the original purposes of a charitable gift can be altered to allow the property given or part of it to be applied cy-près shall be as follows—

(a) where the original purposes, in whole or in part—
(i) have been as far as may be fulfilled; or

(ii) cannot be carried out, or not according to the directions given and to the spirit of the gift; or

(b) where the original purposes provide a use for part only of the property available by virtue of the gift; or

(c) where the property available by virtue of the gift and other property applicable for similar purposes can be more effectively used in conjunction, and to that end can suitably, regard being had to the spirit of the gift, be made applicable to common purposes; or

(d) where the original purposes were laid down by reference to an area which then was but has since ceased to be a unit for some other purpose, or by reference to a class of persons or to an area which has for any reason since ceased to be suitable, regard being had to the spirit of the gift, or to be practical in administering the gift; or

(e) where the original purposes, in whole or in part, have, since they were laid down,—

   (i) been adequately provided for by other means; or

   (ii) ceased, as being useless or harmful to the community or for other reasons, to be in law charitable; or

   (iii) ceased in any other way to provide a suitable and effective method of using the property available by virtue of the gift, regard being had to the spirit of the gift.

(2) Subsection (1) above shall not affect the conditions which must be satisfied in order that property given for charitable purposes may be applied cy-près except in so far as those conditions require a failure of the original purposes.

(3) References in the foregoing subsections to the original purposes of a gift shall be construed, where the application of the property given has been altered or regulated by a scheme or otherwise, as referring to the purposes for which the property is for the time being applicable.

(4) Without prejudice to the power to make schemes in circumstances falling within subsection (1) above, the court may by scheme made under the court's jurisdiction with respect to charities, in any case where the purposes for which the property is held are laid down by reference to any such area as is mentioned in the first column in Schedule 3 to this Act, provide for enlarging the area to any such area as is mentioned in the second column in the same entry in that Schedule.

(5) It is hereby declared that a trust for charitable purposes places a trustee under a duty, where the case permits and requires the property or some part of it to be applied cy-près, to secure its effective use for charity by taking steps to enable it to be so applied.

For a definition of cy-près, see the Introduction.

S.13 – *Extends the circumstances in which the Commission may apply the cy-près principle from those previously used by the Courts. So long as it is clear that the donor had a general charitable intention (even if the proposed methodology is impracticable) the cy-près principle can operate to save the gift which might otherwise have to revert to the donor. In applying the cy-près principle, the Commission tend to be cautious in their approach, perhaps concerned that donors would be less free with giving money to charity if they knew that their stipulations could be easily over-ridden.*

Examples of gifts that might be altered under S.13(1)(a) to (e) could be:-

(a) *a gift to assist soldiers returning from the Crimean War;*

(b) *a gift for poor children in a particular parish, there being insufficient poor families;*

(c) *where two or more charities would act more effectively if amalgamated;*

(d) *a gift for people suffering from an illness which is no longer so common (eg leprosy);*

(e) *a gift to build and maintain a bridge linking two parts of a town, now maintainable on the rates.*

Simpler rules and provisions are available for reorganising small charities – see Ss.74 and 75.

Under S.13(5) trustees have a positive duty to apply for a cy-près scheme where the existing trusts of their charity make effective use of funds impossible.

14 Application cy-près of gifts of donors unknown or disclaiming

(1) Property given for specific charitable purposes which fail shall be applicable cy-près as if given for charitable purposes generally, where it belongs—

    (a) to a donor who after—

        (i) the prescribed advertisements and inquiries have been published and made, and

        (ii) the prescribed period beginning with the publication of those advertisements has expired,

cannot be identified or cannot be found; or

    (b) to a donor who has executed a disclaimer in the prescribed form of his right to have the property returned.

(2) Where the prescribed advertisements and inquiries have been published and made by or on behalf of trustees with respect to any such property, the trustees shall not be liable to any person in respect of the property if no claim by him to be interested in it is received by them before the expiry of the period mentioned in subsection (1)(a)(ii) above.

(3) For the purposes of this section property shall be conclusively presumed (without any advertisement or inquiry) to belong to donors who cannot be identified, in so far as it consists—

(a) of the proceeds of cash collections made by means of collecting boxes or by other means not adapted for distinguishing one gift from another; or

(b) of the proceeds of any lottery, competition, entertainment, sale or similar money-raising activity, after allowing for property given to provide prizes or articles for sale or otherwise to enable the activity to be undertaken.

(4) The court may by order direct that property not falling within subsection (3) above shall for the purposes of this section be treated (without any advertisement or inquiry) as belonging to donors who cannot be identified where it appears to the court either—

(a) that it would be unreasonable, having regard to the amounts likely to be returned to the donors, to incur expense with a view to returning the property; or

(b) that it would be unreasonable, having regard to the nature, circumstances and amounts of the gifts, and to the lapse of time since the gifts were made, for the donors to expect the property to be returned.

(5) Where property is applied cy-près by virtue of this section, the donor shall be deemed to have parted with all his interest at the time when the gift was made; but where property is so applied as belonging to donors who cannot be identified or cannot be found, and is not so applied by virtue of subsection (3) or (4) above—

(a) the scheme shall specify the total amount of that property; and

(b) the donor of any part of that amount shall be entitled, if he makes a claim not later than six months after the date on which the scheme is made, to recover from the charity for which the property is applied a sum equal to that part, less any expenses properly incurred by the charity trustees after that date in connection with claims relating to his gift; and

(c) the scheme may include directions as to the provision to be made for meeting any such claim.

(6) Where—

(a) any sum is, in accordance with any such directions, set aside for meeting any such claims, but

(b) the aggregate amount of any such claims actually made exceeds the relevant amount, then, if the Commissioners so direct, each of the donors in question shall be entitled only to such proportion of the relevant amount as the amount of his claim bears to the aggregate amount referred to in paragraph (b) above; and for this purpose "the relevant amount" means the amount of the sum so set aside after deduction of any expenses properly incurred by the charity trustees in connection with claims relating to the donors' gifts.

(7) For the purposes of this section, charitable purposes shall be deemed to "fail" where any difficulty in applying property to those purposes makes that property or the part not applicable cy-près available to be returned to the donors.

(8) In this section "prescribed" means prescribed by regulations made by the Commissioners; and such regulations may, as respects the advertisements which are to be published for the purposes of subsection (1)(a) above, make provision as to the form and content of such advertisements as well as the manner in which they are to be published.

(9) Any regulations made by the Commissioners under this section shall be published by the Commissioners in such manner as they think fit.

(10) In this section, except in so far as the context otherwise requires, references to a donor include persons claiming through or under the original donor, and references to property given include the property for the time being representing the property originally given or property derived from it.

(11) This section shall apply to property given for charitable purposes, notwithstanding that it was so given before the commencement of this Act.

S.14 – *The general rule is that, if property is given for a very specific charitable purpose which cannot be carried out and no general charitable intent can be implied, the property must be returned to the donor. That may be easy enough if there is one donor but could be a nightmare where there are several, some perhaps unknown or uncontactable.*

In consequence, S.14 allows general charitable intent (and therefore the possibility of a cy-près scheme) to be implied so long as suitable advertisements – S.14(1) – have been placed and either the gifts are disclaimed or the donor cannot be found.

S.14(3) – *Provides that no advertisement is needed where money has been given in lotteries, collecting boxes etc.*

S.14(4) – *Provides that the Court (but not the Commission) can order that donors can be presumed unidentified if sums of money are small or if circumstances make it unreasonable for the money to be returned.*

S.14(5) – *Provides that an untraced donor can within six months of a Commission scheme recover money which would have been returned to him if identified earlier but less the expenses of the trustees.*

S.14(8) – *Provides for regulations to be made regarding advertisements for unknown donors – see Charities (Cy-près Advertisements, Inquiries and Disclaimer) Regulations 1993. These regulations prescribe the form of advertisement, the method of publication, the appropriate time limits and the form of disclaimer for donors wishing to disclaim.*

15 Charities governed by charter, or by or under statute

(1) Where a Royal charter establishing or regulating a body corporate is amendable by the grant and acceptance of a further charter, a scheme relating to the body corporate or to the administration of property held by the body (including a scheme for the cy-près application of any such property) may be made by the court under the court's jurisdiction with respect to charities notwithstanding that the scheme cannot take effect without the alteration of the charter, but shall be so framed that the scheme, or such part of it as cannot take effect without the alteration of the charter, does not purport to come into operation unless or until Her Majesty thinks fit to amend the charter in such manner as will permit the scheme or that part of it to have effect.

(2) Where under the court's jurisdiction with respect to charities or the corresponding jurisdiction of a court in Northern Ireland, or under powers conferred by this Act or by any Northern Ireland legislation relating to charities, a scheme is made with respect to a body corporate, and it appears to Her Majesty expedient, having regard to the scheme, to amend any Royal charter relating to that body, Her Majesty may, on the application of that body, amend the charter accordingly by Order in Council in any way in which the charter could be amended by the grant and acceptance of a further charter; and any such Order in Council may be revoked or varied in like manner as the charter it amends.

(3) The jurisdiction of the court with respect to charities shall not be excluded or restricted in the case of a charity of any description mentioned in Schedule 4 to this Act by the operation of the enactments or instruments there mentioned in relation to that description, and a scheme established for any such charity may modify or supersede in relation to it the provision made by any such enactment or instrument as if made by a scheme of the court, and may also make any such provision as is authorised by that Schedule.

S.15 – *Normally the Court (and therefore the commission) has no power to alter the trusts of a charity founded by Royal Charter. S.15(1) gives jurisdiction to the Court or the Commission to frame a scheme to amend the charter's provisions but subject to approval of Her Majesty the Queen.*

S.15(3) *allows certain charities established by certain statutes set out in Schedule 4 to be amended by the Court or the Commission. See S.17 in relation to all other charities created by statute.*

Powers of Commissioners to make schemes and act for protection of charities etc

16 Concurrent jurisdiction with High Court for certain purposes

(1) Subject to the provisions of this Act, the Commissioners may by order exercise the same jurisdiction and powers as are exercisable by the High Court in charity proceedings for the following purposes—

(a) establishing a scheme for the administration of a charity;

(b) appointing, discharging or removing a charity trustee or trustee for a charity, or removing an officer or employee;

(c) vesting or transferring property, or requiring or entitling any person to call for or make any transfer of property or any payment.

(2) Where the court directs a scheme for the administration of a charity to be established, the court may by order refer the matter to the Commissioners for them to prepare or settle a scheme in accordance with such directions (if any) as the court sees fit to give, and any such order may provide for the scheme to be put into effect by order of the Commissioners as if prepared under subsection (1) above and without any further order of the court.

(3) The Commissioners shall not have jurisdiction under this section to try or determine the title at law or in equity to any property as between a charity or trustee for a charity and a person holding or claiming the property or an interest in it adversely to the charity, or to try or determine any question as to the existence or extent of any charge or trust.

(4) Subject to the following subsections, the Commissioners shall not exercise their jurisdiction under this section as respects any charity, except—

(a) on the application of the charity; or

(b) on an order of the court under subsection (2) above; or

(c) in the case of a charity other than an exempt charity, on the application of the Attorney General.

(5) In the case of a charity which is not an exempt charity and whose income from all sources does not in aggregate exceed £500 a year, the Commissioners may exercise their jurisdiction under this section on the application—

(a) of any one or more of the charity trustees; or

(b) of any person interested in the charity; or

(c) of any two or more inhabitants of the area of the charity if it is a local charity.

(6) Where in the case of a charity, other than an exempt charity, the Commissioners are satisfied that the charity trustees ought in the interests of the charity to apply for a scheme, but have unreasonably refused or neglected to do so and the Commissioners have given the charity trustees an opportunity to make representations to them, the Commissioners may proceed as if an application for a scheme had been made by the charity but the Commissioners shall not have power in a case where they act by virtue of this subsection to alter the purposes of a charity, unless forty years have elapsed from the date of its foundation.

(7) Where—

(a) a charity cannot apply to the Commissioners for a scheme by reason of any vacancy among the charity trustees or the absence or incapacity of any of them, but

(b) such an application is made by such number of the charity trustees as the Commissioners consider appropriate in the circumstances of the case,

the Commissioners may nevertheless proceed as if the application were an application made by the charity.

(8) The Commissioners may on the application of any charity trustee or trustee for a charity exercise their jurisdiction under this section for the purpose of discharging him from his trusteeship.

(9) Before exercising any jurisdiction under this section otherwise than on an order of the court, the Commissioners shall give notice of their intention to do so to each of the charity trustees, except any that cannot be found or has no known address in the United Kingdom or who is party or privy to an application for the exercise of the jurisdiction; and any such notice may be given by post, and, if given by post, may be addressed to the recipient's last known address in the United Kingdom.

(10) The Commissioners shall not exercise their jurisdiction under this section in any case (not referred to them by order of the court) which, by reason of its contentious character, or of any special question of law or of fact which it may involve, or for other reasons, the Commissioners may consider more fit to be adjudicated on by the court.

(11) An appeal against any order of the Commissioners under this section may be brought in the High Court by the Attorney General.

(12) An appeal against any order of the Commissioners under this section may also, at any time within the three months beginning with the day following that on which the order is published, be brought in the High Court by the charity or any of the charity trustees, or by any person removed from any office or employment by the order (unless he is removed with the concurrence of the charity trustees or with the approval of the special visitor, if any, of the charity).

(13) No appeal shall be brought under subsection (12) above except with a certificate of the Commissioners that it is a proper case for an appeal or with the leave of one of the judges of the High Court attached to the Chancery Division.

(14) Where an order of the Commissioners under this section establishes a scheme for the administration of a charity, any person interested in the charity shall have the like right of appeal under subsection (12) above as a charity trustee, and so also, in the case of a charity which is a local charity in any area, shall any two or more inhabitants of the area and the council of any parish or (in Wales) any community comprising the area or any part of it.

(15)   If the Secretary of State thinks it expedient to do so—

(a) in consequence of changes in the value of money, or
(b) with a view to increasing the number of charities in respect of which the Commissioners may exercise their jurisdiction under this section in accordance with subsection (5) above,

he may by order amend that subsection by substituting a different sum for the sum for the time being specified there.

> **S.16** – *Gives the Commission concurrent jurisdiction with the High Court to establish schemes for the administration of a charity, making changes in trustees, vesting charity property. However alteration of charitable purposes can only be dealt with by the Commission under Ss. 13 and 14.*
>
> *Generally the trustees must by majority concur in the application for a scheme but for very small charities lesser rules apply. A scheme can alter both previous Commission schemes and previous administrative provisions.*
>
> *The Commission can send contentious cases to the Court.*

17 Further powers to make schemes or alter application of charitable property

(1) Where it appears to the Commissioners that a scheme should be established for the administration of a charity, but also that it is necessary or desirable for the scheme to alter the provision made by an Act of Parliament establishing or regulating the charity or to make any other provision which goes or might go beyond the powers exercisable by them apart from this section, or that it is for any reason proper for the scheme to be subject to parliamentary review, then (subject to subsection (6) below) the Commissioners may settle a scheme accordingly with a view to its being given effect under this section.

(2) A scheme settled by the Commissioners under this section may be given effect by order of the Secretary of State, and a draft of the order shall be laid before Parliament.

(3) Without prejudice to the operation of section 6 of the Statutory Instruments Act 1946 in other cases, in the case of a scheme which goes beyond the powers exercisable apart from this section in altering a statutory provision contained in or having effect under any public general Act of Parliament, the order shall not be made unless the draft has been approved by resolution of each House of Parliament.

(4) Subject to subsection (5) below, any provision of a scheme brought into effect under this section may be modified or superseded by the court or the Commissioners as if it were a scheme brought into effect by order of the Commissioners under section 16 above.

(5) Where subsection (3) above applies to a scheme, the order giving effect to it may direct that the scheme shall not be modified or superseded by a scheme brought into effect otherwise than under this section, and may also direct that that subsection shall apply to any scheme modifying or superseding the scheme to which the order gives effect.

(6) The Commissioners shall not proceed under this section without the like application and the like notice to the charity trustees, as would be required if they were proceeding (without an order of the court) under section 16 above; but on any application for a scheme, or in a case where they act by virtue of subsection (6) or (7) of that section, the Commissioners may proceed under this section or that section as appears to them appropriate.

(7) Notwithstanding anything in the trusts of a charity, no expenditure incurred in preparing or promoting a Bill in Parliament shall without the consent of the court or the Commissioners be defrayed out of any moneys applicable for the purposes of a charity but this subsection shall not apply in the case of an exempt charity.

(8) Where the Commissioners are satisfied—

    (a) that the whole of the income of a charity cannot in existing circumstances be effectively applied for the purposes of the charity; and

    (b) that, if those circumstances continue, a scheme might be made for applying the surplus cy-près; and

    (c) that it is for any reason not yet desirable to make such a scheme;

then the Commissioners may by order authorise the charity trustees at their discretion (but subject to any conditions imposed by the order) to apply any accrued or accruing income for any purposes for which it might be made applicable by such a scheme, and any application authorised by the order shall be deemed to be within the purposes of the charity.

(9) An order under subsection (8) above shall not extend to more than £300 out of income accrued before the date of the order, nor to income accruing more than three years after that date, nor to more than £100 out of the income accruing in any of those three years.

S.17 – *Provides a procedure whereby charities established by statute (and whose constitution could otherwise only be altered by statute) can nevertheless be altered by Charity Commission scheme.*

Most such statutes will have been private Acts of Parliament and the procedure therefore requires the negative resolution procedure, so that a copy of the proposed Order in Council establishing the scheme is laid before each House of Parliament for a period of 40 days and as long as there has been no negative resolution of either House of Parliament, the order will be enacted and therefore the scheme will come into force after that 40 day period.

For the less common, public general Acts of Parliament a scheme under S.17 will require a positive resolution of each House which obviously takes longer because of the pressure on parliamentary time.

18 Power to act for protection of charities

(1) Where, at any time after they have instituted an inquiry under section 8 above with respect to any charity, the Commissioners are satisfied—

    (a) that there is or has been any misconduct or mismanagement in the administration of the charity; or

    (b) that it is necessary or desirable to act for the purpose of protecting the property of the charity or securing a proper application for the purposes of the charity of that property or of property coming to the charity,

the Commissioners may of their own motion do one or more of the following things—

    (i) by order suspend any trustee, charity trustee, officer, agent or employee of the charity from the exercise of his office or employment pending consideration being given to his removal (whether under this section or otherwise);

    (ii) by order appoint such number of additional charity trustees as they consider necessary for the proper administration of the charity;

    (iii) by order vest any property held by or in trust for the charity in the official custodian, or require the persons in whom any such property is vested to transfer it to him, or appoint any person to transfer any such property to him;

    (iv) order any person who holds any property on behalf of the charity, or of any trustee for it, not to part with the property without the approval of the Commissioners;

    (v) order any debtor of the charity not to make any payment in or towards the discharge of his liability to the charity without the approval of the Commissioners;

    (vi) by order restrict (notwithstanding anything in the trusts of the charity) the transactions which may be entered into, or the nature or amount of the payments which may be made, in the administration of the charity without the approval of the Commissioners;

(vii) by order appoint (in accordance with section 19 below) a receiver and manager in respect of the property and affairs of the charity.

(2) Where, at any time after they have instituted an inquiry under section 8 above with respect to any charity, the Commissioners are satisfied—

(a) that there is or has been any misconduct or mismanagement in the administration of the charity; and

(b) that it is necessary or desirable to act for the purpose of protecting the property of the charity or securing a proper application for the purposes of the charity of that property or of property coming to the charity,

the Commissioners may of their own motion do either or both of the following things—

(i) by order remove any trustee, charity trustee, officer, agent or employee of the charity who has been responsible for or privy to the misconduct or mismanagement or has by his conduct contributed to it or facilitated it;

(ii) by order establish a scheme for the administration of the charity.

(3) The references in subsection (1) or (2) above to misconduct or mismanagement shall (notwithstanding anything in the trusts of the charity) extend to the employment for the remuneration or reward of persons acting in the affairs of the charity, or for other administrative purposes, of sums which are excessive in relation to the property which is or is likely to be applied or applicable for the purposes of the charity.

(4) The Commissioners may also remove a charity trustee by order made of their own motion—

(a) where, within the last five years, the trustee—

(i) having previously been adjudged bankrupt or had his estate sequestrated, has been discharged, or

(ii) having previously made a composition or arrangement with, or granted a trust deed for, his creditors, has been discharged in respect of it;

(b) where the trustee is a corporation in liquidation;

(c) where the trustee is incapable of acting by reason of mental disorder within the meaning of the Mental Health Act 1983;

(d) where the trustee has not acted, and will not declare his willingness or unwillingness to act;

(e) where the trustee is outside England and Wales or cannot be found or does not act, and his absence or failure to act impedes the proper administration of the charity.

(5) The Commissioners may by order made of their own motion appoint a person to be a charity trustee—

    (a) in place of a charity trustee removed by them under this section or otherwise;

    (b) where there are no charity trustees, or where by reason of vacancies in their number or the absence or incapacity of any of their number the charity cannot apply for the appointment;

    (c) where there is a single charity trustee, not being a corporation aggregate, and the Commissioners are of opinion that it is necessary to increase the number for the proper administration of the charity;

    (d) where the Commissioners are of opinion that it is necessary for the proper administration of the charity to have an additional charity trustee because one of the existing charity trustees who ought nevertheless to remain a charity trustee either cannot be found or does not act or is outside England and Wales.

(6) The powers of the Commissioners under this section to remove or appoint charity trustees of their own motion shall include power to make any such order with respect to the vesting in or transfer to the charity trustees of any property as the Commissioners could make on the removal or appointment of a charity trustee by them under section 16 above.

(7) Any order under this section for the removal or appointment of a charity trustee or trustee for a charity, or for the vesting or transfer of any property, shall be of the like effect as an order made under section 16 above.

(8) Subject to subsection (9) below, subsections (11) to (13) of section 16 above shall apply to orders under this section as they apply to orders under that section.

(9) The requirement to obtain any such certificate or leave as is mentioned in section 16(13) above shall not apply to—

    (a) an appeal by a charity or any of the charity trustees of a charity against an order under subsection (1)(vii) above appointing a receiver and manager in respect of the charity's property and affairs, or

    (b) an appeal by a person against an order under subsection (2)(i) or (4)(a) above removing him from his office or employment.

(10) Subsection (14) of section 16 above shall apply to an order under this section which establishes a scheme for the administration of a charity as it applies to such an order under that section.

(11) The power of the Commissioners to make an order under subsection (1)(i) above shall not be exercisable so as to suspend any person from the exercise of his office or employment for a period of more than twelve months; but (without prejudice to the generality of section 89(1) below), any such order made in the case of any person may make provision as respects the period of his suspension for matters arising out of it, and in particular for enabling any person to execute any instrument in his name or otherwise act for him and, in the case of a charity trustee, for adjusting any rules governing the proceedings of the charity trustees to take account of the reduction in the number capable of acting.

(12) Before exercising any jurisdiction under this section otherwise than by virtue of subsection (1) above, the Commissioners shall give notice of their intention to do so to each of the charity trustees, except any that cannot be found or has no known address in the United Kingdom; and any such notice may be given by post and, if given by post, may be addressed to the recipient's last known address in the United Kingdom.

(13) The Commissioners shall, at such intervals as they think fit, review any order made by them under paragraph (i), or any of paragraphs (iii) to (vii), of subsection (1) above; and, if on any such review it appears to them that it would be appropriate to discharge the order in whole or in part, they shall so discharge it (whether subject to any savings or other transitional provisions or not).

(14) If any person contravenes an order under subsection (1)(iv), (v) or (vi) above, he shall be guilty of an offence and liable on summary conviction to a fine not exceeding level 5 on the standard scale.

(15) Subsection (14) above shall not be taken to preclude the bringing of proceedings for breach of trust against any charity trustee or trustee for a charity in respect of a contravention of an order under subsection (1)(iv) or (vi) above (whether proceedings in respect of the contravention are brought against him under subsection (14) above or not).

(16) This section shall not apply to an exempt charity.

S.18 – *Gives the Commission particular powers, which it exercises through its Investigation Division, to act for the protection of a charity or its property, but only when S.8 Inquiry - see S.8 above - has been established. However, there need be no delay between the establishment of an Inquiry and the use of S.18 powers.*

*Under S18(1) if they are satisfied **either** of misconduct or mismanagement in the charity **or** that they should act for the protection or proper application of assets of the charity, the Commission can exercise their S.18 powers which include:-*

- *suspension of a trustee, employee or agent of the charity (the suspension being limited to 12 months).*

- *vesting charity property in the Official Custodian*

- *freezing assets and bank accounts*

- *restricting the charity's transactions*

- *appointing a Receiver and Manager under S.19*

S.18(2) – *Provides that if the Commission are satisfied **both** that there has been misconduct or mismanagement **and** that they should act for the protection or proper application of the charity assets, then they can also remove (as distinct from suspend) a trustee, employee or agent of the charity or establish a scheme for administration of the charity. In other words where permanent remedial powers are exercised, the Commission has to have stronger grounds.*

There are provisions for appeal to the High Court against orders made by the Commission under this section.

S.18(4) & (5) *also give the commission powers to remove trustees who are bankrupt or uncapable or unwilling to act and to appoint additional or replacement trustees.*

S.18(14) – *Underpins the orders to freeze property and bank accounts and to restrict transactions by creating a criminal offence for breach.*

19 Supplementary provisions relating to receiver and manager appointed for a charity

(1) The Commissioners may under section 18(1)(vii) above appoint to be receiver and manager in respect of the property and affairs of a charity such person (other than an officer or employee of theirs) as they think fit.

(2) Without prejudice to the generality of section 89(1) below, any order made by the Commissioners under section 18(1)(vii) above may make provision with respect to the functions to be discharged by the receiver and manager appointed by the order; and those functions shall be discharged by him under the supervision of the Commissioners.

(3) In connection with the discharge of those functions any such order may provide—

(a) for the receiver and manager appointed by the order to have such powers and duties of the charity trustees of the charity concerned (whether arising under this Act or otherwise) as are specified in the order;

(b) for any powers or duties exercisable or falling to be performed by the receiver and manager by virtue of paragraph (a) above to be exercisable or performed by him to the exclusion of those trustees.

(4) Where a person has been appointed receiver and manager by any such order—

(a) section 29 below shall apply to him and to his functions as a person so appointed as it applies to a charity trustee of the charity concerned and to his duties as such; and

(b) the Commissioners may apply to the High Court for directions in relation to any particular matter arising in connection with the discharge of those functions.

(5) The High Court may on an application under subsection (4)(b) above—

    (a) give such directions, or

    (b) make such orders declaring the rights of any persons (whether before the court or not),

as it thinks just; and the costs of any such application shall be paid by the charity concerned.

(6) Regulations made by the Secretary of State may make provision with respect to—

    (a) the appointment and removal of persons appointed in accordance with this section;

    (b) the remuneration of such persons out of the income of the charities concerned;

    (c) the making of reports to the Commissioners by such persons.

(7) Regulations under subsection (6) above may, in particular, authorise the Commissioners—

    (a) to require security for the due discharge of his functions to be given by a person so appointed;

    (b) to determine the amount of such a person's remuneration;

    (c) to disallow any amount of remuneration in such circumstances as are prescribed by the regulations.

S.19 – *Makes provision for the appointment of a Receiver and Manager under S.18(1)(vii). The Receiver and Manager's powers and duties are specified by the Commission and he can be given advice but he is independent of the Commission. At the time of publication the Commission have made 25 appointments of Receivers and Managers.*

The Charities (Receiver and Manager) Regulations 1991 (SI. No. 2355) have been made under this section, but they give the Receiver and Manager no more guidance than can be gleaned from the Act.

In general the commission's order appointing the Receiver and manager will appoint him effectively to act as the sole trustee of the charity until he has completed his duties – eg to restructure or wind up the charity.

20 Publicity for proceedings under ss 16 to 18

(1) The Commissioners shall not make any order under this Act to establish a scheme for the administration of a charity, or submit such a scheme to the court or the Secretary of State for an order giving it effect, unless not less than one month previously there has been given public notice of their proposals, inviting

representations to be made to them within a time specified in the notice, being not less than one month from the date of such notice, and, in the case of a scheme relating to a local charity, other than on ecclesiastical charity, in a parish or (in Wales) a community, a draft of the scheme has been communicated to the parish or community council or, in the case of a parish not having a council, to the chairman of the parish meeting.

(2) The Commissioners shall not make any order under this Act to appoint, discharge or remove a charity trustee or trustee for a charity (other than the official custodian), unless not less than one month previously there has been given the like public notice as is required by subsection (1) above for an order establishing a scheme but this subsection shall not apply in the case of—

(a) an order under section 18(1)(ii) above; or
(b) an order discharging or removing a trustee if the Commissioners are of opinion that it is unnecessary and not in his interest to give publicity to the proposal to discharge or remove him.

(3) Before the Commissioners make an order under this Act to remove without his consent a charity trustee or trustee for a charity, or an officer, agent or employee of a charity, the Commissioners shall, unless he cannot be found or has no known address in the United Kingdom, give him not less than one month's notice of their proposal, inviting representations to be made to them within a time specified in the notice.

(4) Where notice is given of any proposals as required by subsections (1) to (3) above, the Commissioners shall take into consideration any representations made to them about the proposals within the time specified in the notice, and may (without further notice) proceed with the proposals either without modification or with such modifications as appear to them to be desirable.

(5) Where the Commissioners make an order which is subject to appeal under subsection (12) of section 16 above the order shall be published either by giving public notice of it or by giving notice of it to all persons entitled to appeal against it under that subsection, as the Commissioners think fit.

(6) Where the Commissioners make an order under this Act to establish a scheme for the administration of a charity, a copy of the order shall, for not less than one month after the order is published, be available for public inspection at all reasonable times at the Commissioners' office and also at some convenient place in the area of the charity, if it is a local charity.

(7) Any notice to be given under this section of any proposals or order shall give such particulars of the proposals or order, or such directions for obtaining information about them, as the Commissioners think sufficient and appropriate, and any public notice shall be given in such manner as they think sufficient and appropriate.

(8) Any notice to be given under this section, other than a public notice, may be given by post and, if given by post, may be addressed to the recipient's last known address in the United Kingdom.

> **S.20** – *Requires the Commission to give one month's public notice of any proposed scheme under Ss.16-18. The same applies to orders relating to the appointment, discharge or removal of trustees. Furthermore, the Commission must make an attempt to give personal notice of its proposed removal of a trustee, employee or agent of the charity.*

Property vested in official custodian

21 Entrusting charity property to official custodian, and termination of trust

(1) The court may by order—

   (a) vest in the official custodian any land held by or in trust for a charity;
   (b) authorise or require the persons in whom any such land is vested to transfer it to him; or
   (c) appoint any person to transfer any such land to him;

but this subsection does not apply to any interest in land by way of mortgage or other security.

(2) Where property is vested in the official custodian in trust for a charity, the court may make an order discharging him from the trusteeship as respects all or any of that property.

(3) Where the official custodian is discharged from his trusteeship of any property, or the trusts on which he holds any property come to an end, the court may make such vesting orders and give such directions as may seem to the court to be necessary or expedient in consequence.

(4) No person shall be liable for any loss occasioned by his acting in conformity with an order under this section or by his giving effect to anything done in pursuance of such an order, or be excused from so doing by reason of the order having been in any respect improperly obtained.

> **S.21** – *Allows the Court to order that a charity's property is vested in the Official Custodian for Charities.*

22 Supplementary provisions as to property vested in official custodian

(1) Subject to the provisions of this Act, where property is vested in the official custodian in trust for a charity, he shall not exercise any powers of management, but he shall as trustee of any property have all the same powers, duties and liabilities, and be entitled to the same rights and immunities, and be subject to the control and orders of the court, as a corporation appointed custodian trustee under section 4 of the Public Trustee Act 1906 except that he shall have no power to charge fees.

(2) Subject to subsection (3) below, where any land is vested in the official custodian in trust for a charity, the charity trustees shall have power in his name and on his behalf to execute and do all assurances and things which they could properly execute or do in their own name and on their own behalf if the land were vested in them.

(3) If any land is so vested in the official custodian by virtue of an order under section 18 above, the power conferred on the charity trustees by subsection (2) above shall not be exercisable by them in relation to any transaction affecting the land, unless the transaction is authorised by order of the court or of the Commissioners.

(4) Where any land is vested in the official custodian in trust for a charity, the charity trustees shall have the like power to make obligations entered into by them binding on the land as if it were vested in them; and any covenant, agreement or condition which is enforceable by or against the custodian by reason of the land being vested in him shall be enforceable by or against the charity trustees as if the land were vested in them.

(5) In relation to a corporate charity, subsections (2), (3) and (4) above shall apply with the substitution of references to the charity for references to the charity trustees.

(6) Subsections (2), (3) and (4) above shall not authorise any charity trustees or charity to impose any personal liability on the official custodian.

(7) Where the official custodian is entitled as trustee for a charity to the custody of securities or documents of title relating to the trust property, he may permit them to be in the possession or under the control of the charity trustees without thereby incurring any liability.

S.22 – *Confirms that the Official Custodian, like any custodian trustee, has no powers of management of a charity, as such powers remain in the hands of the charity trustees. That is not necessarily the case if land has been vested in the Official Custodian by the Commission under the protective powers of S.18.*

23 Divestment in the case of land subject to Reverter of Sites Act 1987

(1) Where—

(a) any land is vested in the official custodian in trust for a charity, and

(b) it appears to the Commissioners that section 1 of the Reverter of Sites Act 1987 (right of reverter replaced by [trust]) will, or is likely to, operate in relation to the land at a particular time or in particular circumstances,

the jurisdiction which, under section 16 above, is exercisable by the Commissioners for the purpose of discharging a trustee for a charity may, at any time before section 1 of that Act ("the 1987 Act") operates in relation to the land, be exercised by them of their own motion for the purpose of—

(i) making an order discharging the official custodian from his trusteeship of the land, and

(ii) making such vesting orders and giving such directions as appear to them to be necessary or expedient in consequence.

(2) Where—

(a) section 1 of the 1987 Act has operated in relation to any land which, immediately before the time when that section so operated, was vested in the official custodian in trust for a charity, and

(b) the land remains vested in him but on the trust arising under that section,

the court or the Commissioners (of their own motion) may—

(i) make an order discharging the official custodian from his trusteeship of the land, and

(ii) (subject to the following provisions of this section) make such vesting orders and give such directions as appear to it or them to be necessary or expedient in consequence.

(3) Where any order discharging the official custodian from his trusteeship of any land—

(a) is made by the court under section 21(2) above, or by the Commissioners under section 16 above, on the grounds that section 1 of the 1987 Act will, or is likely to, operate in relation to the land, or

(b) is made by the court or the Commissioners under subsection (2) above,

the persons in whom the land is to be vested on the discharge of the official custodian shall be the relevant charity trustees (as defined in subsection (4) below), unless the court or (as the case may be) the Commissioners is or are satisfied that it would be appropriate for it to be vested in some other persons.

(4) In subsection (3) above "the relevant charity trustees" means—

(a) in relation to an order made as mentioned in paragraph (a) of that subsection, the charity trustees of the charity in trust for which the land is vested in the official custodian immediately before the time when the order takes effect, or

(b) in relation to an order made under subsection (2) above, the charity trustees of the charity in trust for which the land was vested in the official custodian immediately before the time when section 1 of the 1987 Act operated in relation to the land.

(5) Where—

(a) section 1 of the 1987 Act has operated in relation to any such land as is mentioned in subsection (2)(a) above, and

(b) the land remains vested in the official custodian as mentioned in subsection (2)(b) above,

then (subject to subsection (6) below), all the powers, duties and liabilities that would, apart from this section, be those of the official custodian as [trustee] of the land shall instead be those of the charity trustees of the charity concerned; and those trustees shall have power in his name and on his behalf to execute and do all assurances and things which they could properly execute or do in their own name and on their own behalf if the land were vested in them.

(6) Subsection (5) above shall not be taken to require or authorise those trustees to sell the land at a time when it remains vested in the official custodian.

(7) Where—

(a) the official custodian has been discharged from his trusteeship of any land by an order under subsection (2) above, and

(b) the land has, in accordance with subsection (3) above, been vested in the charity trustees concerned or (as the case may be) in any persons other than those trustees,

the land shall be held by those trustees, or (as the case may be) by those persons, as [trustees] on the terms of the trust arising under section 1 of the 1987 Act.

(8) The official custodian shall not be liable to any person in respect of any loss or misapplication of any land vested in him in accordance with that section unless it is occasioned by or through any wilful neglect or default of his or of any person acting for him; but the Consolidated Fund shall be liable to make good to any person any sums for which the official custodian may be liable by reason of any such neglect or default.

(9) In this section any reference to section 1 of the 1987 Act operating in relation to any land is a reference to a [trust] arising in relation to the land under that section.

S.23 – *Allows the Commission to order that property held in the rather special circumstances of the Reverter of Sites Act 1987, where there has been a failure of the charitable purpose, should be transferred by the Official Custodian to other trustees.*

Establishment of common investment or deposit funds

24 Schemes to establish common investment funds

(1) The court or the Commissioners may by order make and bring into effect schemes (in this section referred to as "common investment schemes") for the establishment of common investment funds under trusts which provide—

   (a) for property transferred to the fund by or on behalf of a charity participating in the scheme to be invested under the control of trustees appointed to manage the fund; and

   (b) for the participating charities to be entitled (subject to the provisions of the scheme) to the capital and income of the fund in shares determined by reference to the amount or value of the property transferred to it by or on behalf of each of them and to the value of the fund at the time of the transfers.

(2) The court or the Commissioners may make a common investment scheme on the application of any two or more charities.

(3) A common investment scheme may be made in terms admitting any charity to participate, or the scheme may restrict the right to participate in any manner.

(4) A common investment scheme may make provision for, and for all matters connected with, the establishment, investment, management and winding up of the common investment fund, and may in particular include provision—

   (a) for remunerating persons appointed trustees to hold or manage the fund or any part of it, with or without provision authorising a person to receive the remuneration notwithstanding that he is also a charity trustee of or trustee for a participating charity;

   (b) for restricting the size of the fund, and for regulating as to time, amount or otherwise the right to transfer property to or withdraw it from the fund, and for enabling sums to be advanced out of the fund by way of loan to a participating charity pending the withdrawal of property from the fund by the charity;

   (c) for enabling income to be withheld from distribution with a view to avoiding fluctuations in the amounts distributed, and generally for regulating distributions of income;

   (d) for enabling money to be borrowed temporarily for the purpose of meeting payments to be made out of the funds;

   (e) for enabling questions arising under the scheme as to the right of a charity to participate, or as to the rights of participating charities, or as to any other matter, to be conclusively determined by the decision of the trustees managing the fund or in any other manner;

   (f) for regulating the accounts and information to be supplied to participating charities.

(5) A common investment scheme, in addition to the provision for property to be transferred to the fund on the basis that the charity shall be entitled to a share in the capital and income of the fund, may include provision for enabling sums to be

deposited by or on behalf of a charity on the basis that (subject to the provisions of the scheme) the charity shall be entitled to repayment of the sums deposited and to interest thereon at a rate determined by or under the scheme; and where a scheme makes any such provision it shall also provide for excluding from the amount of capital and income to be shared between charities participating otherwise than by way of deposit such amounts (not exceeding the amounts properly attributable to the making of deposits) as are from time to time reasonably required in respect of the liabilities of the fund for the repayment of deposits and for the interest on deposits, including amounts required by way of reserve.

(6) Except in so far as a common investment scheme provides to the contrary, the rights under it of a participating charity shall not be capable of being assigned or charged, nor shall any trustee or other person concerned in the management of the common investment fund be required or entitled to take account of any trust or other equity affecting a participating charity or its property or rights.

(7) The powers of investment of every charity shall include power to participate in common investment schemes unless the power is excluded by a provision specifically referring to common investment schemes in the trusts of the charity.

(8) A common investment fund shall be deemed for all purposes to be a charity; and if the scheme admits only exempt charities, the fund shall be an exempt charity for the purposes of this Act.

(9) Subsection (8) above shall apply not only to common investment funds established under the powers of this section, but also to any similar fund established for the exclusive benefit of charities by or under any enactment relating to any particular charities or class of charity.

S.24 – *Re-enacts the power of the Commission under the Charities Act 1960 to establish common investment funds, particularly following the policy decision to dispense with the investment-holding role of the Official Custodian.*

Obtaining investment advice (which charity trustees are bound to do) and a good return on capital can be expensive for the smaller charity and the Commission encourages them to invest with appropriate advice by collecting together and establishing common investment funds (under S.24) and common deposit funds (under S.25) to pool investments. Common investment funds are themselves charities. For example the Charities Official Investment Fund (COIF) was established by a scheme in 1962.

Under S.24(7) all charities can participate in common investment schemes unless specifically prevented from doing so by their constitution.

Under S.24(8) a common investment fund is a charity and registerable by the Commission, though if it only admits exempt charities, it would itself be an exempt charity.

25 Schemes to establish common deposit funds

(1) The court or the Commissioners may by order make and bring into effect schemes (in this section referred to as "common deposit schemes") for the establishment of common deposit funds under trusts which provide—

    (a) for sums to be deposited by or on behalf of a charity participating in the scheme and invested under the control of trustees appointed to manage the fund; and

    (b) for any such charity to be entitled (subject to the provisions of the scheme) to repayment of any sums so deposited and to interest thereon at a rate determined under the scheme.

(2) Subject to subsection (3) below, the following provisions of section 24 above, namely—

    (a) subsections (2) to (4), and

    (b) subsections (6) to (9),

shall have effect in relation to common deposit schemes and common deposit funds as they have effect in relation to common investment schemes and common investment funds.

(3) In its application in accordance with subsection (2) above, subsection (4) of that section shall have effect with the substitution for paragraphs (b) and (c) of the following paragraphs—

    "(b) for regulating as to time, amount or otherwise the right to repayment of sums deposited in the fund;

    (c) for authorising a part of the income for any year to be credited to a reserve account maintained for the purpose of counteracting any losses accruing to the fund, and generally for regulating the manner in which the rate of interest on deposits is to be determined from time to time;".

> **S.25** – *In similar fashion to S.24 common deposit funds can be established by two or more charities. For instance COIF established the Charities Fixed Interest and Deposit Fund via a Charity Commission scheme in 1989.*

Additional powers of Commissioners

26 Power to authorise dealings with charity property etc

(1) Subject to the provisions of this section, where it appears to the Commissioners that any action proposed or contemplated in the administration of a charity is expedient in the interests of the charity, they may by order sanction that action,

whether or not it would otherwise be within the powers exercisable by the charity trustees in the administration of the charity; and anything done under the authority of such an order shall be deemed to be properly done in the exercise of those powers.

(2) An order under this section may be made so as to authorise a particular transaction, compromise or the like, or a particular application of property, or so as to give a more general authority, and (without prejudice to the generality of subsection (1) above) may authorise a charity to use common premises, or employ a common staff, or otherwise combine for any purpose of administration, with any other charity.

(3) An order under this section may give directions as to the manner in which any expenditure is to be borne and as to other matters connected with or arising out of the action thereby authorised; and where anything is done in pursuance of an authority given by any such order, any directions given in connection therewith shall be binding on the charity trustees for the time being as if contained in the trusts of the charity; but any such directions may on the application of the charity be modified or superseded by a further order.

(4) Without prejudice to the generality of subsection (3) above, the directions which may be given by an order under this section shall in particular include directions for meeting any expenditure out of a specified fund, for charging any expenditure to capital or to income, for requiring expenditure charged to capital to be recouped out of income within a specified period, for restricting the costs to be incurred at the expense of the charity, or for the investment of moneys arising from any transaction.

(5) An order under this section may authorise any act notwithstanding that it is prohibited by any of the disabling Acts mentioned in subsection (6) below or that the trusts of the charity provide for the act to be done by or under the authority of the court; but no such order shall authorise the doing of any act expressly prohibited by Act of Parliament other than the disabling Acts or by the trusts of the charity or shall extend or alter the purposes of the charity.

(6) The Acts referred to in subsection (5) above as the disabling Acts are the Ecclesiastical Leases Act 1571, the Ecclesiastical Leases Act 1572, the Ecclesiastical Leases Act 1575 and the Ecclesiastical Leases Act 1836.

(7) An order under this section shall not confer any authority in relation to a building which has been consecrated and of which the use or disposal is regulated, and can be further regulated, by a scheme having effect under the Union of Benefices Measures 1923 to 1952, the Reorganisation Areas Measures 1944 and 1954, the Pastoral Measure 1968 or the Pastoral Measure 1983, the reference to a building being taken to include part of a building and any land which under such a scheme is to be used or disposed of with a building to which the scheme applies.

S.26 – *This much-used section allows the Commission to authorise action falling within a charity's objects but not permitted by the charity's constitution.*

The action to be authorised has to be "expedient in the interests" of the charity. Examples of orders regularly made by the Commission under this section are:

- *permitting discretionary investment management and investments to be held in nominee names*

- *authorising the use of permanently endowed capital*

- *authorising a payment to a charity's trading subsidiary.*

- *authorising trustee indemnity insurance*

- *authorising a payment to a charity's trustee*

27 Power to authorise ex gratia payments etc

(1) Subject to subsection (3) below, the Commissioners may by order exercise the same power as is exercisable by the Attorney General to authorise the charity trustees of a charity—

    (a) to make any application of property of the charity, or

    (b) to waive to any extent, on behalf of the charity, its entitlement to receive any property,

in a case where the charity trustees—

    (i) (apart from this section) have no power to do so, but

    (ii) in all the circumstances regard themselves as being under a moral obligation to do so.

(2) The power conferred on the Commissioners by subsection (1) above shall be exercisable by them under the supervision of, and in accordance with such directions as may be given by, the Attorney General; and any such directions may in particular require the Commissioners, in such circumstances as are specified in the directions—

    (a) to refrain from exercising that power; or

    (b) to consult the Attorney General before exercising it.

(3) Where—

    (a) an application is made to the Commissioners for them to exercise that power in a case where they are not precluded from doing so by any such directions, but

    (b) they consider that it would nevertheless be desirable for the application to be entertained by the Attorney General rather than by them,

they shall refer the application to the Attorney General.

(4) It is hereby declared that where, in the case of any application made to them as mentioned in subsection (3)(a) above, the Commissioners determine the application by refusing to authorise charity trustees to take any action falling within subsection (1)(a) or (b) above, that refusal shall not preclude the Attorney General, on an application subsequently made to him by the trustees, from authorising the trustees to take that action.

S.27 – *Allows the Commission to authorise ex gratia payments where there is a moral imperative. Previously the Attorney General had had the sole power of authorising ex gratia payments but he now has a supervisory role. Examples of the use of this power are:-*

* *payment of pension to long-serving employees where there is no contractual right to the pension*

* *waiving the right to receive all or part of a gift under a will when there is a moral obligation to a testator's family falling short of a legal right to the testator's money or property.*

28 Power to give directions about dormant bank accounts of charities

(1) Where the Commissioners—

    (a) are informed by a relevant institution—
        (i) that it holds one or more accounts in the name of or on behalf of a particular charity ("the relevant charity"), and
        (ii) that the account, or (if it so holds two or more accounts) each of the accounts, is dormant, and
    (b) are unable, after making reasonable inquiries, to locate that charity or any of its trustees,

they may give a direction under subsection (2) below.

(2) A direction under this subsection is a direction which—

    (a) requires the institution concerned to transfer the amount, or (as the case may be) the aggregate amount, standing to the credit of the relevant charity in the account or accounts in question to such other charity as is specified in the direction in accordance with subsection (3) below; or
    (b) requires the institution concerned to transfer to each of two or more other charities so specified in the direction such part of that amount or aggregate amount as is there specified in relation to that charity.

(3) The Commissioners may specify in a direction under subsection (2) above such other charity or charities as they consider appropriate, having regard, in a case where the purposes of the relevant charity are known to them, to those purposes

and to the purposes of the other charity or charities; but the Commissioners shall not so specify any charity unless they have received from the charity trustees written confirmation that those trustees are willing to accept the amount proposed to be transferred to the charity.

(4) Any amount received by a charity by virtue of this section shall be received by the charity on terms that—

(a) it shall be held and applied by the charity for the purposes of the charity, but

(b) it shall, as property of the charity, nevertheless be subject to any restrictions on expenditure to which it was subject as property of the relevant charity.

(5) Where—

(a) the Commissioners have been informed as mentioned in subsection (1)(a) above by any relevant institution, and

(b) before any transfer is made by the institution in pursuance of a direction under subsection (2) above, the institution has, by reason of any circumstances, cause to believe that the account, or (as the case may be) any of the accounts, held by it in the name of or on behalf of the relevant charity is no longer dormant,

the institution shall forthwith notify those circumstances in writing to the Commissioners; and, if it appears to the Commissioners that the account or accounts in question is or are no longer dormant, they shall revoke any direction under subsection (2) above which has previously been given by them to the institution with respect to the relevant charity.

(6) The receipt of any charity trustees or trustee for a charity in respect of any amount received from a relevant institution by virtue of this section shall be a complete discharge of the institution in respect of that amount.

(7) No obligation as to secrecy or other restriction on disclosure (however imposed) shall preclude a relevant institution from disclosing any information to the Commissioners for the purpose of enabling them to discharge their functions under this section.

(8) For the purposes of this section—

(a) an account is dormant if no transaction, other than—

(i) a transaction consisting in a payment into the account, or

(ii) a transaction which the institution holding the account has itself caused to be effected,

has been effected in relation to the account within the period of five years immediately preceding the date when the Commissioners are informed as mentioned in paragraph (a) of subsection (1) above;

(b) a "relevant institution" means—

(i) the Bank of England;

(ii) an institution which is authorised by the [Financial Services Authority] to operate a deposit-taking business under Part I of the Banking Act 1987;

(iii) a European deposit-taker as defined in regulation 82(3) of the Banking Coordination (Second Council Directive) Regulations 1992;

(iv) a building society which is authorised by the Building Societies Commission under section 9 of the Building Societies Act 1986 to raise money from its members; or

(v) such other institution mentioned in Schedule 2 to the Banking Act 1987 as the Secretary of State may prescribe by regulations; and

(c) references to the transfer of any amount to a charity are references to its transfer—

(i) to the charity trustees, or

(ii) to any trustee for the charity,

as the charity trustees may determine (and any reference to any amount received by a charity shall be construed accordingly).

(9) For the purpose of determining the matters in respect of which any of the powers conferred by section 8 or 9 above may be exercised it shall be assumed that the Commissioners have no functions under this section in relation to accounts to which this subsection applies (with the result that, for example, a relevant institution shall not, in connection with the functions of the Commissioners under this section, be required under section 8(3)(a) above to furnish any statements, or answer any questions or inquiries, with respect to any such accounts held by the institution).

This subsection applies to accounts which are dormant accounts by virtue of subsection (8)(a) above but would not be such accounts if sub-paragraph (i) of that provision were omitted.

(10) Subsection (1) above shall not apply to any account held in the name of or on behalf of an exempt charity.

S.28 – *Allows dormant bank and building society accounts to be paid to another charity where the owning charity or its trustees cannot be located. The chief condition is that the money is not used by the receiving charity for 5 years.*

29 Power to advise charity trustees

(1) The Commissioners may on the written application of any charity trustee give him their opinion or advice on any matter affecting the performance of his duties as such.

(2) A charity trustee or trustee for a charity acting in accordance with the opinion or advice of the Commissioners given under this section with respect to the charity shall be deemed, as regards his responsibility for so acting, to have acted in accordance with his trust, unless, when he does so, either—

(a) he knows or has reasonable cause to suspect that the opinion or advice was given in ignorance of material facts; or

(b) the decision of the court has been obtained on the matter or proceedings are pending to obtain one.

S.29 – *This is a short but useful provision allowing the Commissioners to advise trustees what they should do in particular circumstances, provided that the Commission are given sufficient evidence. If the trustees follow that advice, then they are protected unless they have misled the Commission. The advice is free and is therefore a useful alternative to asking the Court for a decision but in practice S.29 advice is only given where the Commission believe that what they are advising does in fact come within the powers of the trusts of the charity – i.e. it is not an alternative to an order under S.26; nor is it always an alternative to obtaining appropriate professional advice.*

30 Powers for preservation of charity documents

(1) The Commissioners may provide books in which any deed, will or other document relating to a charity may be enrolled.

(2) The Commissioners may accept for safe keeping any document of or relating to a charity, and the charity trustees or other persons having the custody of documents of or relating to a charity (including a charity which has ceased to exist) may with the consent of the Commissioners deposit them with the Commissioners for safe keeping, except in the case of documents required by some other enactment to be kept elsewhere.

(3) Where a document is enrolled by the Commissioners or is for the time being deposited with them under this section, evidence of its contents may be given by means of a copy certified by any officer of the Commissioners generally or specially authorised by them to act for this purpose; and a document purporting to be such a copy shall be received in evidence without proof of the official position, authority or handwriting of the person certifying it or of the original document being enrolled or deposited as aforesaid.

(4) Regulations made by the Secretary of State may make provision for such documents deposited with the Commissioners under this section as may be prescribed by the regulations to be destroyed or otherwise disposed of after such period or in such circumstances as may be so prescribed.

(5) Subsections (3) and (4) above shall apply to any document transmitted to the Commissioners under section 9 above and kept by them under subsection (3) of that section, as if the document had been deposited with them for safe keeping under this section.

S.30 – *Allows the Commission to "enrol" documents relating to a charity and to accept documents for safe keeping. Regulations for enrolment could be made by the Home Secretary but have not been and in practice these provisions are little publicised and little used because trustees rightly see safekeeping of their documents as part of their own responsibility. It would be unusual now for the Commission to accept documents for enrolment or for safekeeping.*

31 Power to order taxation of solicitor's bill

(1) The Commissioners may order that a solicitor's bill of costs for business done for a charity, or for charity trustees or trustees for a charity, shall be taxed, together with the costs of the taxation, by a taxing officer in such division of the High Court as may be specified in the order, or by the taxing officer of any other court having jurisdiction to order the taxation of the bill.

(2) On any order under this section for the taxation of a solicitor's bill the taxation shall proceed, and the taxing officer shall have the same powers and duties, and the costs of the taxation shall be borne, as if the order had been made, on the application of the person chargeable with the bill, by the court in which the costs are taxed.

(3) No order under this section for the taxation of a solicitor's bill shall be made after payment of the bill unless the Commissioners are of opinion that it contains exorbitant charges; and no such order shall in any case be made where the solicitor's costs are not subject to taxation on an order of the High Court by reason either of an agreement as to his remuneration or the lapse of time since payment of the bill.

S.31 – *Allows the Commission to order that a solicitor's bill for a charity can be "taxed" (checked by the Court) if it is considered exorbitant.*

Legal proceedings relating to charities

32 Proceedings by Commissioners

(1) Subject to subsection (2) below, the Commissioners may exercise the same powers with respect to—

  (a) the taking of legal proceedings with reference to charities or the property or affairs of charities, or

(b) the compromise of claims with a view to avoiding or ending such proceedings,

as are exercisable by the Attorney General acting ex officio.

(2) Subsection (1) above does not apply to the power of the Attorney General under section 63(1) below to present a petition for the winding up of a charity.

(3) The practice and procedure to be followed in relation to any proceedings taken by the Commissioners under subsection (1) above shall be the same in all respects (and in particular as regards costs) as if they were proceedings taken by the Attorney General acting ex officio.

(4) No rule of law or practice shall be taken to require the Attorney General to be a party to any such proceedings.

(5) The powers exercisable by the Commissioners by virtue of this section shall be exercisable by them of their own motion, but shall be exercisable only with the agreement of the Attorney General on each occasion.

> **S.32** – *Gives the Commission the same powers to take legal proceedings in relation to charities as the Attorney General can take, other than the winding up of charity (see S.63(1)).*

33 Proceedings by other persons

(1) Charity proceedings may be taken with reference to a charity either by the charity, or by any of the charity trustees, or by any person interested in the charity, or by any two or more inhabitants of the area of the charity if it is a local charity, but not by any other person.

(2) Subject to the following provisions of this section, no charity proceedings relating to a charity (other than an exempt charity) shall be entertained or proceeded with in any court unless the taking of the proceedings is authorised by order of the Commissioners.

(3) The Commissioners shall not, without special reasons, authorise the taking of charity proceedings where in their opinion the case can be dealt with by them under the powers of this Act other than those conferred by section 32 above.

(4) This section shall not require any order for the taking of proceedings in a pending cause or matter or for the bringing of any appeal.

(5) Where the foregoing provisions of this section require the taking of charity proceedings to be authorised by an order of the Commissioners, the proceedings may nevertheless be entertained or proceeded with if, after the order had been applied for and refused, leave to take the proceedings was obtained from one of the judges of the High Court attached to the Chancery Division.

(6) Nothing in the foregoing subsections shall apply to the taking of proceedings by the Attorney General, with or without a relator, or to the taking of proceedings by the Commissioners in accordance with section 32 above.

(7) Where it appears to the Commissioners, on an application for an order under this section or otherwise, that it is desirable for legal proceedings to be taken with reference to any charity (other than an exempt charity) or its property or affairs, and for the proceedings to be taken by the Attorney General, the Commissioners shall so inform the Attorney General, and send him such statements and particulars as they think necessary to explain the matter.

(8) In this section "charity proceedings" means proceedings in any court in England or Wales brought under the court's jurisdiction with respect to charities, or brought under the court's jurisdiction with respect to trusts in relation to the administration of a trust for charitable purposes.

> **S.33** – *Provides for the authority of the Commission to be obtained before any charity proceedings can be commenced. "Charity proceedings" are those which involve the administration or carrying out of charitable trusts involving either the trustees or interested persons – the latter has been held to include parents of an independent school under threat of closure where the trustees' decision-making process was questioned.*
>
> *However, "charity proceedings" do not include litigation by or against a charity in contractual matters or enforcement of property or common law rights, for which no authority is required from the Commission.*
>
> *The point of this section is that the Commission may well be able to deal with an administrative dispute more economically in time and money than would be the case if the matter were taken to the High Court.*

34 Report of s 8 inquiry to be evidence in certain proceedings

(1) A copy of the report of the person conducting an inquiry under section 8 above shall, if certified by the Commissioners to be a true copy, be admissible in any proceedings to which this section applies—

(a) as evidence of any fact stated in the report; and
(b) as evidence of the opinion of that person as to any matter referred to in it.

(2) This section applies to—

(a) any legal proceedings instituted by the Commissioners under this Part of this Act; and
(b) any legal proceedings instituted by the Attorney General in respect of a charity.

(3) A document purporting to be a certificate issued for the purposes of subsection (1) above shall be received in evidence and be deemed to be such a certificate, unless the contrary is proved.

S.34 – *Allows reports of S.8 Inquiries to be produced as evidence, thus obviating the need for direct proof by the person who wrote the report.*

Meaning of "trust corporation"

35 Application of provisions to trust corporations appointed under s 16 or 18

(1) In the definition of "trust corporation" contained in the following provisions—

    (a) section 117(xxx) of the Settled Land Act 1925,
    (b) section 68(18) of the Trustee Act 1925,
    (c) section 205(xxviii) of the Law of Property Act 1925,
    (d) section 55(xxvi) of the Administration of Estates Act 1925, and
    (e) section 128 of the Supreme Court Act 1981,

the reference to a corporation appointed by the court in any particular case to be a trustee includes a reference to a corporation appointed by the Commissioners under this Act to be a trustee.

(2) This section shall be deemed always to have had effect; but the reference to section 128 of the Supreme Court Act 1981 shall, in relation to any time before 1st January 1982, be construed as a reference to section 175(1) of the Supreme Court of Judicature (Consolidation) Act 1925.

S.35 – *Confirms that a trust corporation appointed by the Commission to be a trustee has the same rights and obligations as one appointed by the Court.*

PART V
CHARITY LAND

36 Restrictions on dispositions

(1) Subject to the following provisions of this section and section 40 below, no land held by or in trust for a charity shall be sold, leased or otherwise disposed of without an order of the court or of the Commissioners.

(2) Subsection (1) above shall not apply to a disposition of such land if—

(a) the disposition is made to a person who is not—
    (i) a connected person (as defined in Schedule 5 to this Act), or
    (ii) a trustee for, or nominee of, a connected person; and
(b) the requirements of subsection (3) or (5) below have been complied with in relation to it.

(3) Except where the proposed disposition is the granting of such a lease as is mentioned in subsection (5) below, the charity trustees must, before entering into an agreement for the sale, or (as the case may be) for a lease or other disposition, of the land—

(a) obtain and consider a written report on the proposed disposition from a qualified surveyor instructed by the trustees and acting exclusively for the charity;
(b) advertise the proposed disposition for such period and in such manner as the surveyor has advised in his report (unless he has there advised that it would not be in the best interests of the charity to advertise the proposed disposition); and
(c) decide that they are satisfied, having considered the surveyor's report, that the terms on which the disposition is proposed to be made are the best that can reasonably be obtained for the charity.

(4) For the purposes of subsection (3) above a person is a qualified surveyor if—

(a) he is a fellow or professional associate of the Royal Institution of Chartered Surveyors or of the Incorporated Society of Valuers and Auctioneers or satisfies such other requirement or requirements as may be prescribed by regulations made by the Secretary of State; and
(b) he is reasonably believed by the charity trustees to have ability in, and experience of, the valuation of land of the particular kind, and in the particular area, in question;

and any report prepared for the purposes of that subsection shall contain such information, and deal with such matters, as may be prescribed by regulations so made.

(5) Where the proposed disposition is the granting of a lease for a term ending not more than seven years after it is granted (other than one granted wholly or partly in consideration of a fine), the charity trustees must, before entering into an agreement for the lease—

(a) obtain and consider the advice on the proposed disposition of a person who is reasonably believed by the trustees to have the requisite ability and practical experience to provide them with competent advice on the proposed disposition; and
(b) decide that they are satisfied, having considered that person's advice, that the terms on which the disposition is proposed to be made are the best that can reasonably be obtained for the charity.

(6) Where—

    (a) any land is held by or in trust for a charity, and

    (b) the trusts on which it is so held stipulate that it is to be used for the purposes, or any particular purposes, of the charity,

then (subject to subsections (7) and (8) below and without prejudice to the operation of the preceding provisions of this section) the land shall not be sold, leased or otherwise disposed of unless the charity trustees have previously—

    (i) given public notice of the proposed disposition, inviting representations to be made to them within a time specified in the notice, being not less than one month from the date of the notice; and

    (ii) taken into consideration any representations made to them within that time about the proposed disposition.

(7) Subsection (6) above shall not apply to any such disposition of land as is there mentioned if—

    (a) the disposition is to be effected with a view to acquiring by way of replacement other property which is to be held on the trusts referred to in paragraph (b) of that subsection; or

    (b) the disposition is the granting of a lease for a term ending not more than two years after it is granted (other than one granted wholly or partly in consideration of a fine).

(8) The Commissioners may direct—

    (a) that subsection (6) above shall not apply to dispositions of land held by or in trust for a charity or class of charities (whether generally or only in the case of a specified class of dispositions or land, or otherwise as may be provided in the direction), or

    (b) that that subsection shall not apply to a particular disposition of land held by or in trust for a charity,

if, on an application made to them in writing by or on behalf of the charity or charities in question, the Commissioners are satisfied that it would be in the interests of the charity or charities for them to give the direction.

(9) The restrictions on disposition imposed by this section apply notwithstanding anything in the trusts of a charity; but nothing in this section applies—

    (a) to any disposition for which general or special authority is expressly given (without the authority being made subject to the sanction of an order of the court) by any statutory provision contained in or having effect under an Act of Parliament or by any scheme legally established; or

    (b) to any disposition of land held by or in trust for a charity which—

        (i) is made to another charity otherwise than for the best price that can reasonably be obtained, and

(ii) is authorised to be so made by the trusts of the first-mentioned charity; or

(c) to the granting, by or on behalf of a charity and in accordance with its trusts, of a lease to any beneficiary under those trusts where the lease—

(i) is granted otherwise than for the best rent that can reasonably be obtained; and

(ii) is intended to enable the demised premises to be occupied for the purposes, or any particular purposes, of the charity.

(10)   Nothing in this section applies—

(a) to any disposition of land held by or in trust for an exempt charity;

(b) to any disposition of land by way of mortgage or other security; or

(c) to any disposition of an advowson.

(11)   In this section "land" means land in England or Wales.

S.36 – *Prior to the 1992 Act charities were generally required to obtain Charity Commission consent for selling, leasing or otherwise disposing of charity land. Now, provided that a charity which wants to dispose of land obtains advice from a qualified surveyor and follows his advice on marketing the land in a procedure under S.36(3), designed to obtain the best terms for any disposal, the consent of the Commission to the disposal is not required.*

As the whole intention of S.36 is to dispose of property on the best terms that can reasonably be obtained for the charity, the Commission is unlikely to give consent for any disposal outside the S.36(3) procedure other than in exceptional circumstances; even then, they would require a surveyor's report.

Note that "the best terms" would usually mean accepting the highest price, but that is not always the case and other conditions of disposal should also be considered if they benefit the charity.

Consent of the Commission to a disposal is always required if the sale is to a "connected person" (as to which see Schedule 5), for example a trustee, employee or agent of the charity or their close relatives; a connected person includes a charity's non-charitable trading subsidiary.

There are variations or exceptions to the S.36(3) procedure:-

- *Under S.36(5) a lease for less than 7 years requires advice from a person of ability and practical experience, so not necessarily a qualified surveyor.*

- *Under S.36(6) where land is held on special trusts requiring it to be used for the purposes of the charity (e.g. an almshouse) one month's prior public notice must be given, in addition to following the S.36(3) or S.36(5) procedures.*

- *Under S.36(9)(b) and (c) disposals to similar charities or to beneficiaries of the charity do not require the disposal procedures or the consent of the Charity Commission.*

S.36(10) provides that S.36 does not apply to an exempt charity or to the mortgage of land – mortgages are dealt with under S.38.

37 Supplementary provisions relating to dispositions

(1) Any of the following instruments, namely—

- (a) any contract for the sale, or for a lease or other disposition, of land which is held by or in trust for a charity, and
- (b) any conveyance, transfer, lease or other instrument effecting a disposition of such land,

shall state—

- (i) that the land is held by or in trust for a charity,
- (ii) whether the charity is an exempt charity and whether the disposition is one falling within paragraph (a), (b) or (c) of subsection (9) of section 36 above, and
- (iii) if it is not an exempt charity and the disposition is not one falling within any of those paragraphs, that the land is land to which the restrictions on disposition imposed by that section apply.

(2) Where any land held by or in trust for a charity is sold, leased or otherwise disposed of by a disposition to which subsection (1) or (2) of section 36 above applies, the charity trustees shall certify in the instrument by which the disposition is effected—

- (a) (where subsection (1) of that section applies) that the disposition has been sanctioned by an order of the court or of the Commissioners (as the case may be), or
- (b) (where subsection (2) of that section applies) that the charity trustees have power under the trusts of the charity to effect the disposition, and that they have complied with the provisions of that section so far as applicable to it.

(3) Where subsection (2) above has been complied with in relation to any disposition of land, then in favour of a person who (whether under the disposition or afterwards) acquires an interest in the land for money or money's worth, it shall be conclusively presumed that the facts were as stated in the certificate.

(4) Where—

- (a) any land held by or in trust for a charity is sold, leased or otherwise disposed of by a disposition to which subsection (1) or (2) of section 36 above applies, but

(b) subsection (2) above has not been complied with in relation to the disposition,

then in favour of a person who (whether under the disposition or afterwards) in good faith acquires an interest in the land for money or money's worth, the disposition shall be valid whether or not—

    (i) the disposition has been sanctioned by an order of the court or of the Commissioners, or

    (ii) the charity trustees have power under the trusts of the charity to effect the disposition and have complied with the provisions of that section so far as applicable to it.

(5) Any of the following instruments, namely—

    (a) any contract for the sale, or for a lease or other disposition, of land which will, as a result of the disposition, be held by or in trust for a charity, and

    (b) any conveyance, transfer, lease or other instrument effecting a disposition of such land,

shall state—

    (i) that the land will, as a result of the disposition, be held by or in trust for a charity,

    (ii) whether the charity is an exempt charity, and

    (iii) if it is not an exempt charity, that the restrictions on disposition imposed by section 36 above will apply to the land (subject to subsection (9) of that section).

(6) . . .

(7) Where—

    (a) the disposition to be effected by any such instrument as is mentioned in subsection (1)(b) or (5)(b) above will be a registered disposition, or

    (b) any such instrument will on taking effect be an instrument [in relation to which section 123A] of the Land Registration Act 1925 (compulsory registration of title) applies,

the statement which, by virtue of subsection (1) or (5) above, is to be contained in the instrument shall be in such form as may be prescribed.

(8) Where—

    (a) an application is duly made—

        (i) for registration of a disposition of registered land, or

        (ii) for registration of a person's title under a disposition of unregistered land, and

    (b) the instrument by which the disposition is effected contains a statement complying with subsections (5) and (7) above, and

    (c) the charity by or in trust for which the land is held as a result of the disposition is not an exempt charity, the registrar shall enter in the register, in respect of the land, a restriction in such form as may be prescribed.

(9) Where—

    (a) any such restriction is entered in the register in respect of any land, and

    (b) the charity by or in trust for which the land is held becomes an exempt charity,

the charity trustees shall apply to the registrar for the restriction to be withdrawn; and on receiving any application duly made under this subsection the registrar shall withdraw the restriction.

(10)   Where—

    (a) any registered land is held by or in trust for an exempt charity and the charity ceases to be an exempt charity, or

    (b) any registered land becomes, as a result of a declaration of trust by the registered proprietor, land held in trust for a charity (other than an exempt charity),

the charity trustees shall apply to the registrar for such a restriction as is mentioned in subsection (8) above to be entered in the register in respect of the land; and on receiving any application duly made under this subsection the registrar shall enter such a restriction in the register in respect of the land.

(11)   In this section—

    (a) references to a disposition of land do not include references to—

        (i) a disposition of land by way of mortgage or other security,

        (ii) any disposition of an advowson, or

        (iii) any release of a rentcharge failing within section 40(1) below; and

    (b) "land" means land in England or Wales;

and subsections (7) to (10) above shall be construed as one with the Land Registration Act 1925.

S.37 – *To ensure compliance with S.36, all charities (whether or not exempt) are required to make statements in contracts, transfers, leases and the like to alert those dealing with them in any transaction as to whether or not the S.36 regime applies and affects the land disposed of or acquired.*

The form of statement or certificate is now specified in the Land Registration (Charities) Rules 1992 (SI.3005).

S.37(4) – *Even where the charity has not complied with S.36, a person who acquired the land for value and acted in good faith is protected.*

38 Restrictions on mortgaging

(1) Subject to subsection (2) below, no mortgage of land held by or in trust for a charity shall be granted without an order of the court or of the Commissioners.

(2) Subsection (1) above shall not apply to a mortgage of any such land by way of security for the repayment of a loan where the charity trustees have, before executing the mortgage, obtained and considered proper advice, given to them in writing, on the matters mentioned in subsection (3) below.

(3) Those matters are—

 (a) whether the proposed loan is necessary in order for the charity trustees to be able to pursue the particular course of action in connection with which the loan is sought by them;

 (b) whether the terms of the proposed loan are reasonable having regard to the status of the charity as a prospective borrower; and

 (c) the ability of the charity to repay on those terms the sum proposed to be borrowed.

(4) For the purposes of subsection (2) above proper advice is the advice of a person—

 (a) who is reasonably believed by the charity trustees to be qualified by his ability in and practical experience of financial matters; and

 (b) who has no financial interest in the making of the loan in question;

and such advice may constitute proper advice for those purposes notwithstanding that the person giving it does so in the course of his employment as an officer or employee of the charity or of the charity trustees.

(5) This section applies notwithstanding anything in the trusts of a charity; but nothing in this section applies to any mortgage for which general or special authority is given as mentioned in section 36(9)(a) above.

(6) In this section—

 "land" means land in England or Wales;
 "mortgage" includes a charge.

(7) Nothing in this section applies to an exempt charity.

> **S.38** – *Provides a regime similar to S.36 for charities in the process of granting mortgages, but the written advice which has to be considered by the trustees must be from someone who has no financial interest in making the loan and whom the trustees believe to be qualified by ability and practical experience in financial matters; this could include an employee of the charity, such as a finance director or bursar, but outside professional advice should be obtained in large or complicated transactions.*

39 Supplementary provisions relating to mortgaging

(1) Any mortgage of land held by or in trust for a charity shall state—

- (a) that the land is held by or in trust for a charity,
- (b) whether the charity is an exempt charity and whether the mortgage is one falling within subsection (5) of section 38 above, and
- (c) if it is not an exempt charity and the mortgage is not one falling within that subsection, that the mortgage is one to which the restrictions imposed by that section apply;

and where the mortgage will be a registered disposition any such statement shall be in such form as may be prescribed.

[(1A) Where any such mortgage will be one falling within section 123(2) of the Land Registration Act 1925—

- (a) the statement required by subsection (1) above shall be in such form as may be prescribed; and
- (b) if the charity is not an exempt charity, the mortgage shall also contain a statement, in such form as may be prescribed, that the restrictions on disposition imposed by section 36 above apply to the land (subject to subsection (9) of that section).

(1B) Where—

- (a) an application is duly made for registration of a person's title to land in connection with such a mortgage as is mentioned in subsection (1A) above, and
- (b) the mortgage contains statements complying with subsections (1) and (1A) above, and
- (c) the charity is not an exempt charity,

the registrar shall enter in the register, in respect of the land, a restriction in such form as may be prescribed; and section 37(9) above shall apply in relation to any such restriction as it applies in relation to one entered in pursuance of section 37(8).]

(2) Where subsection (1) or (2) of section 38 above applies to any mortgage of land held by or in trust for a charity, the charity trustees shall certify in the mortgage—

- (a) (where subsection (1) of that section applies) that the mortgage has been sanctioned by an order of the court or of the Commissioners (as the case may be), or
- (b) (where subsection (2) of that section applies) that the charity trustees have power under the trusts of the charity to grant the mortgage, and that they have obtained and considered such advice as is mentioned in that subsection.

(3) Where subsection (2) above has been complied with in relation to any mortgage, then in favour of a person who (whether under the mortgage or afterwards) acquires an interest in the land in question for money or money's worth, it shall be conclusively presumed that the facts were as stated in the certificate.

(4) Where—

(a) subsection (1) or (2) of section 38 above applies to any mortgage of land held by or in trust for a charity, but

(b) subsection (2) above has not been complied with in relation to the mortgage,

then in favour of a person who (whether under the mortgage or afterwards) in good faith acquires an interest in the land for money or money's worth, the mortgage shall be valid whether or not—

(i) the mortgage has been sanctioned by an order of the court or of the Commissioners, or

(ii) the charity trustees have power under the trusts of the charity to grant the mortgage and have obtained and considered such advice as is mentioned in subsection (2) of that section.

(5) . . .

(6) In this section—

"mortgage" includes a charge, and "mortgagee" shall be construed accordingly; "land" means land in England or Wales;

[and subsections (1) to (1B) above shall be construed as one with the Land Registration Act 1925].

> **S.39** – *Similar "flagging procedures" to S.37 are required in respect of mortgage and similar protection is available for a lender who has acted in good faith.*

40 Release of charity rentcharges

(1) Section 36(1) above shall not apply to the release by a charity of a rentcharge which it is entitled to receive if the release is given in consideration of the payment of an amount which is not less than ten times the annual amount of the rentcharge.

(2) Where a charity which is entitled to receive a rentcharge releases it in consideration of the payment of an amount not exceeding £500, any costs incurred by the charity in connection with proving its title to the rentcharge shall be recoverable by the charity from the person or persons in whose favour the rentcharge is being released.

(3) Neither section 36(1) nor subsection (2) above applies where a rentcharge which a charity is entitled to receive is redeemed under sections 8 to 10 of the Rentcharges Act 1977.

(4) The Secretary of State may by order amend subsection (2) above by substituting a different sum for the sum for the time being specified there.

S.40 – *Provides a special regime for the redemption (in return for a capital sum) of rentcharges receivable by charities from a landowner. In practice this section is unlikely to apply because most rentcharges are redeemed via the compulsory procedure run by the Department of the Environment (DETR) under the Rentcharges Act 1977.*

PART VI
CHARITY ACCOUNTS, REPORTS AND RETURNS

Note
Ss. 41 and 42 apply both to registered and excepted charities but not to exempt charities as to which see S.46. The regime for charitable companies is prescribed by Schedule 4 of the Companies Act 1985 and charitable companies do not have to produce separate sets of accounts to comply with Ss. 41-44.

41 Duty to keep accounting records

(1) The charity trustees of a charity shall ensure that accounting records are kept in respect of the charity which are sufficient to show and explain all the charity's transactions, and which are such as to—

    (a) disclose at any time, with reasonable accuracy, the financial position of the charity at that time, and

    (b) enable the trustees to ensure that, where any statements of accounts are prepared by them under section 42(1) below, those statements of accounts comply with the requirements of regulations under that provision.

(2) The accounting records shall in particular contain—

    (a) entries showing from day to day all sums of money received and expended by the charity, and the matters in respect of which the receipt and expenditure takes place; and

    (b) a record of the assets and liabilities of the charity.

(3) The charity trustees of a charity shall preserve any accounting records made for the purposes of this section in respect of the charity for at least six years from the end of the financial year of the charity in which they are made.

(4) Where a charity ceases to exist within the period of six years mentioned in subsection (3) above as it applies to any accounting records, the obligation to preserve those records in accordance with that subsection shall continue to be discharged by the last charity trustees of the charity, unless the Commissioners consent in writing to the records being destroyed or otherwise disposed of.

(5) Nothing in this section applies to a charity which is a company.

> **S.41** – *All registered and excepted charities, regardless of size, have to keep (and keep up to date) accounting records to show their current financial position and enable annual accounts to be prepared in the required form. Records must be kept for at least 6 years. The requirement is to be able to show and explain all the charity's transactions and that includes special trusts and the activities of a charity's branches.*

42 Annual statements of accounts

(1) The charity trustees of a charity shall (subject to subsection (3) below) prepare in respect of each financial year of the charity a statement of accounts complying with such requirements as to its form and contents as may be prescribed by regulations made by the Secretary of State.

(2) Without prejudice to the generality of subsection (1) above, regulations under that subsection may make provision—

  (a) for any such statement to be prepared in accordance with such methods and principles as are specified or referred to in the regulations;
  (b) as to any information to be provided by way of notes to the accounts;

and regulations under that subsection may also make provision for determining the financial years of a charity for the purposes of this Act and any regulations made under it.

(3) Where a charity's gross income in any financial year does not exceed [£100,000], the charity trustees may, in respect of that year, elect to prepare the following, namely—

  (a) a receipts and payments account, and
  (b) a statement of assets and liabilities,

instead of a statement of accounts under subsection (1) above.

(4) The charity trustees of a charity shall preserve—

  (a) any statement of accounts prepared by them under subsection (1) above, or
  (b) any account and statement prepared by them under subsection (3) above,

for at least six years from the end of the financial year to which any such statement relates or (as the case may be) to which any such account and statement relate.

(5) Subsection (4) of section 41 above shall apply in relation to the preservation of any such statement or account and statement as it applies in relation to the preservation of any accounting records (the references to subsection (3) of that section being read as references to subsection (4) above).

(6) The Secretary of State may by order amend subsection (3) above by substituting a different sum for the sum for the time being specified there.

(7) Nothing in this section applies to a charity which is a company.

> **S.42** – *The accounts of a registered or excepted charity have to be in prescribed form and that is contained in the regulations made under S.44 which became effective for accounting periods commencing 1ˢᵗ March 1996. Best practice in the preparation of accounts is contained in the Statement of Recommended Practice for Charity Accounts ("the SORP") which is currently being reviewed.*
>
> **S.42(3)** – *Provides that where a charity's gross income is under £100,000 it has only to submit a receipts and payments account and a statement of assets and liabilities.*

43 Annual audit or examination of charity accounts

(1) Subsection (2) below applies to a financial year of a charity ("the relevant year") if the charity's gross income or total expenditure in any of the following, namely—

   (a) the relevant year,
   (b) the financial year of the charity immediately preceding the relevant year (if any), and
   (c) the financial year of the charity immediately preceding the year specified in paragraph (b) above (if any),

exceeds [£250,000].

(2) If this subsection applies to a financial year of a charity, the accounts of the charity for that year shall be audited by a person who—

   (a) is, in accordance with section 25 of the Companies Act 1989 (eligibility for appointment), eligible for appointment as a company auditor, or
   (b) is a member of a body for the time being specified in regulations under section 44 below and is under the rules of that body eligible for appointment as auditor of the charity.

(3) If subsection (2) above does not apply to a financial year of a charity [and its gross income or total expenditure in that year exceeds £10,000], then (subject to subsection (4) below) the accounts of the charity for that year shall, at the election of the charity trustees, either—

   (a) be examined by an independent examiner, that is to say an independent person who is reasonably believed by the trustees to have the requisite ability and practical experience to carry out a competent examination of the accounts, or
   (b) be audited by such a person as is mentioned in subsection (2) above.

(4) Where it appears to the Commissioners—

(a) that subsection (2), or (as the case may be) subsection (3) above, has not been complied with in relation to a financial year of a charity within ten months from the end of that year, or

(b) that, although subsection (2) above does not apply to a financial year of a charity, it would nevertheless be desirable for the accounts of the charity for that year to be audited by such a person as is mentioned in that subsection,

the Commissioners may by order require the accounts of the charity for that year to be audited by such a person as is mentioned in that subsection.

(5) If the Commissioners make an order under subsection (4) above with respect to a charity, then unless—

(a) the order is made by virtue of paragraph (b) of that subsection, and

(b) the charity trustees themselves appoint an auditor in accordance with the order,

the auditor shall be a person appointed by the Commissioners.

(6) The expenses of any audit carried out by an auditor appointed by the Commissioners under subsection (5) above, including the auditor's remuneration, shall be recoverable by the Commissioners—

(a) from the charity trustees of the charity concerned, who shall be personally liable, jointly and severally, for those expenses; or

(b) to the extent that it appears to the Commissioners not to be practical to seek recovery of those expenses in accordance with paragraph (a) above, from the funds of the charity.

(7) The Commissioners may—

(a) give guidance to charity trustees in connection with the selection of a person for appointment as an independent examiner;

(b) give such directions as they think appropriate with respect to the carrying out of an examination in pursuance of subsection (3)(a) above;

and any such guidance or directions may either be of general application or apply to a particular charity only.

(8) The Secretary of State may by order amend subsection (1) [or (3)] above by substituting a different sum for the sum for the time being specified there.

(9) Nothing in this section applies to a charity which is a company.

Annual Accounts

S.43 – *Provides for an annual audit or independent examinations according to a charity's gross income or expenditure:-*

Income/Expenditure	Requirement (not for Companies)
Below £10,000	*Not usually*
Below £100,000	*Independent examination*
Below £250,000	*Recommendation that independent examiner is a qualified accountant*
Above £250,000	*Professional audit*

While S.43 does not apply to a charitable company it may be helpful to set out here the thresholds under the Companies Act 1985 (Audit Exemption) Regulations 1994 (SI.935) in relation to the company's gross income or expenditure:-

Income/Expenditure	Requirement for Companies
Below £90,000	*A company may claim audit exemption*
Below £250,000	*Report from an independent accountant following examination if audit not required by constitution*
Above £250,000	*Professional audit*

S.43(3) – *Provides that the experience and qualifications of the independent examiner must be considered in relation to the size and complexity of the charity.*

S.43(4) – *Provides that the Commission may order that the accounts of a charity be audited if they consider it desirable.*

S.43(6) – *Provides for the cost of an audit under S.43(4) to be chargeable to the charity trustees themselves or to the charity, at the option of the Commission.*

44 Supplementary provisions relating to audits etc

(1) The Secretary of State may by regulations make provision—

    (a) specifying one or more bodies for the purposes of section 43(2)(b) above;

    (b) with respect to the duties of an auditor carrying out an audit under section 43 above, including provision with respect to the making by him of a report on—

        (i) the statement of accounts prepared for the financial year in question under section 42(1) above, or

        (ii) the account and statement so prepared under section 42(3) above,

    as the case may be;

    (c) with respect to the making by an independent examiner of a report in respect of an examination carried out by him under section 43 above;

    (d) conferring on such an auditor or on an independent examiner a right of access with respect to books, documents and other records (however kept) which relate to the charity concerned;

(e) entitling such an auditor or an independent examiner to require, in the case of a charity, information and explanations from past or present charity trustees or trustees for the charity, or from past or present officers or employees of the charity;

(f) enabling the Commissioners, in circumstances specified in the regulations, to dispense with the requirements of section 43(2) or (3) above in the case of a particular charity or in the case of any particular financial year of a charity.

(2) If any person fails to afford an auditor or an independent examiner any facility to which he is entitled by virtue of subsection (1)(d) or (e) above, the Commissioners may by order give—

(a) to that person, or
(b) to the charity trustees for the time being of the charity concerned,

such directions as the Commissioners think appropriate for securing that the default is made good.

(3) Section 727 of the Companies Act 1985 (power of court to grant relief in certain cases) shall have effect in relation to an auditor or independent examiner appointed by a charity in pursuance of section 43 above as it has effect in relation to a person employed as auditor by a company within the meaning of that Act.

> **S.44** – *Allows regulations to be made to make audits and independent examinations more efficient and effective. These have indeed been made by the Home Secretary in exercise of the powers conferred on him under Ss.42, 44, 45 and 86(3) and are the Charities (Accounts and Reports) Regulations 1995 (SI. 2724).*
>
> **S.44(3)** – *Also allows the Court to give an auditor or examiner relief from liability if he has acted honestly and reasonably and ought to be excused.*

45 Annual reports

(1) The charity trustees of a charity shall prepare in respect of each financial year of the charity an annual report containing—

(a) such a report by the trustees on the activities of the charity during that year, and
(b) such other information relating to the charity or to its trustees or officers,

as may be prescribed by regulations made by the Secretary of State.

(2) Without prejudice to the generality of subsection (1) above, regulations under that subsection may make provision—

(a) for any such report as is mentioned in paragraph (a) of that subsection to be prepared in accordance with such principles as are specified or referred to in the regulations;

(b) enabling the Commissioners to dispense with any requirement prescribed by virtue of subsection (1)(b) above in the case of a particular charity or a particular class of charities, or in the case of a particular financial year of a charity or of any class of charities.

(3) [Where in any financial year of a charity its gross income or total expenditure exceeds £10,000, the annual report required to be prepared under this section in respect of that year] shall be transmitted to the Commissioners by the charity trustees—

(a) within ten months from the end of that year, or

(b) within such longer period as the Commissioners may for any special reason allow in the case of that report.

[(3A) Where in any financial year of a charity neither its gross income nor its total expenditure exceeds £10,000, the annual report required to be prepared under this section in respect of that year shall, if the Commissioners so request, be transmitted to them by the charity trustees—

(a) in the case of a request made before the end of seven months from the end of the financial year to which the report relates, within ten months from the end of that year, and

(b) in the case of a request not so made, within three months from the date of the request,

or, in either case, within such longer period as the Commissioners may for any special reason allow in the case of that report.]

(4) Subject to subsection (5) below, [any annual report transmitted to the Commissioners under this section] shall have attached to it the statement of accounts prepared for the financial year in question under section 42(1) above or (as the case may be) the account and statement so prepared under section 42(3) above, together with—

(a) where the accounts of the charity for that year have been audited under section 43 above, a copy of the report made by the auditor on that statement of accounts or (as the case may be) on that account and statement;

(b) where the accounts of the charity for that year have been examined under section 43 above, a copy of the report made by the independent examiner in respect of the examination carried out by him under that section.

(5) Subsection (4) above does not apply to a charity which is a company, and any annual report transmitted by the charity trustees of such a charity under [this

section] shall instead have attached to it a copy of the charity's annual accounts prepared for the financial year in question under Part VII of the Companies Act 1985, together with a copy of [any auditors' report or report made for the purposes of section 249A(2) of that Act] on those accounts.

(6) Any annual report transmitted to the Commissioners under [this section], together with the documents attached to it, shall be kept by the Commissioners for such period as they think fit.

[(7) The charity trustees of a charity shall preserve, for at least six years from the end of the financial year to which it relates, any annual report prepared by them under subsection (1) above which they have not been required to transmit to the Commissioners.

(8) Subsection (4) of section 41 above shall apply in relation to the preservation of any such annual report as it applies in relation to the preservation of any accounting records (the references in subsection (3) of that section being read as references to subsection (7) above).

(9) The Secretary of State may by order amend subsection (3) or (3A) above by substituting a different sum for the sum for the time being specified there.]

Annual Reports

S.45 – *Requires trustees to produce annual reports detailing the charity's activities for the year in question and other information prescribed by regulation and this information must be sent to the Commission within ten months of the year end, failure to do so being a criminal offence. Again, the requirements, which in this case do apply to charitable companies, increase with the size of the charity's gross income and expenditure:-*

Income and Expenditure Limit	**Requirement**
Below £10,000	*Only if required by the Commission but*
Below £100,000	*must keep the report available for 6 years.*
	Brief summary of main activities and
	achievements of the charity plus standard
	details about the charity including:-
	• *Name and charity number, plus company number if appropriate*
	• *Principal address*
	• *Description of the objects*
	• *Names of trustees*

Income and Expenditure Limit	Requirement
Above £100,000	*Review of all activities, including material transactions and significant developments and achievements, considered in relation to its objects, significant changes in activities in the year, important events and likely future developments PLUS similar details as for a charity below £100,000 but in addition a description of the organisational structure and a description of the charity's assets and arrangements for holding them, (e.g. the storage of deeds and share certificates).*

The Annual Report must, when sent to the Commission be accompanied by the Annual Reports for the financial year in question.

46 Special provision as respects accounts and annual reports of exempt and other excepted charities

(1) Nothing in sections 41 to 45 above applies to any exempt charity; but the charity trustees of an exempt charity shall keep proper books of account with respect to the affairs of the charity, and if not required by or under the authority of any other Act to prepare periodical statements of account shall prepare consecutive statements of account consisting on each occasion of an income and expenditure account relating to a period of not more than fifteen months and a balance sheet relating to the end of that period.

(2) The books of accounts and statements of account relating to an exempt charity shall be preserved for a period of six years at least unless the charity ceases to exist and the Commissioners consent in writing to their being destroyed or otherwise disposed of.

(3) Nothing in sections 43 to 45 above applies to any charity which—

(a) falls within section 3(5)(c) above, and
(b) is not registered.

(4) Except in accordance with subsection (7) below, nothing in section 45 above applies to any charity (other than an exempt charity or a charity which falls within section 3(5)(c) above) which—

(a) is excepted by section 3(5) above, and
(b) is not registered.

(5) If requested to do so by the Commissioners, the charity trustees of any such charity as is mentioned in subsection (4) above shall prepare an annual report in respect of such financial year of the charity as is specified in the Commissioners' request.

(6) Any report prepared under subsection (5) above shall contain—

    (a) such a report by the charity trustees on the activities of the charity during the year in question, and

    (b) such other information relating to the charity or to its trustees or officers,

as may be prescribed by regulations made under section 45(1) above in relation to annual reports prepared under that provision.

(7) Subsections (3) to (6) of section 45 [(as originally enacted)] above shall apply to any report required to be prepared under subsection (5) above as if it were an annual report required to be prepared under subsection (1) of that section.

(8) Any reference in this section to a charity which falls within section 3(5)(c) above includes a reference to a charity which falls within that provision but is also excepted from registration by section 3(5)(b) above.

S.46(1) – *Provides that exempt charities should keep accounting records and ensures (unless they are required to do so by other statutes) that they prepare regular financial accounts.*

S.46(3) – *Provides that if a small charity (no permanent endowment or use or occupation of land and income below £1,000 p.a.) chooses to register with the Commission, then the report and accounts regime in Ss.43-45 apply to it.*

S.46(4) – *Provides that an excepted charity does not have to produce an annual report if it is not registered.*

S.46(5) – *Allows the Commission to require such charity to prepare an annual report (which under S.46(6) may have to contain accounts).*

47 Public inspection of annual reports etc

(1) Any annual report or other document kept by the Commissioners in pursuance of section 45(6) above shall be open to public inspection at all reasonable times—

    (a) during the period for which it is so kept; or

    (b) if the Commissioners so determine, during such lesser period as they may specify.

(2) Where any person—

    (a) requests the charity trustees of a charity in writing to provide him with a copy of the charity's most recent accounts, and

(b) pays them such reasonable fee (if any) as they may require in respect of the costs of complying with the request,

those trustees shall comply with the request within the period of two months beginning with the date on which it is made.

(3) In subsection (2) above the reference to a charity's most recent accounts is—

(a) . . .

(b) in the case of [a charity other than one falling within paragraph (c) or (d) below], a reference to the statement of accounts or account and statement prepared in pursuance of section 42(1) or (3) above in respect of the last financial year of the charity in respect of which a statement of accounts or account and statement has or have been so prepared;

[(c) in the case of a charity which is a company, a reference to the most recent annual accounts of the company prepared under Part VII of the Companies Act 1985 in relation to which any of the following conditions is satisfied—

(i) they have been audited;

(ii) a report required for the purposes of section 249A(2) of that Act has been made in respect of them; or

(iii) they relate to a year in respect of which the company is exempt from audit by virtue of section 249A(1) of that Act; and]

(d) in the case of an exempt charity, a reference to the accounts of the charity most recently audited in pursuance of any statutory or other requirement or, if its accounts are not required to be audited, the accounts most recently prepared in respect of the charity.

S.47 – *All annual accounts and reports held by the Commission are open to public inspection. Furthermore, within two months of being requested in writing to do so, any charity (including exempt and excepted charities) must send accounts to a person who has made a written request for them and has paid a reasonable fee. Failure to do so is a criminal offence - see S.49.*

48 Annual returns by registered charities

(1) [Subject to subsection (1A) below,] every registered charity shall prepare in respect of each of its financial years an annual return in such form, and containing such information, as may be prescribed by regulations made by the Commissioners.

[(1A) Subsection (1) above shall not apply in relation to any financial year of a charity in which neither the gross income nor the total expenditure of the charity exceeds £10,000.]

(2) Any such return shall be transmitted to the Commissioners by the date by which the charity trustees are, by virtue of section 45(3) above, required to transmit to them the annual report required to be prepared in respect of the financial year in question.

(3) The Commissioners may dispense with the requirements of subsection (1) above in the case of a particular charity or a particular class of charities, or in the case of a particular financial year of a charity or of any class of charities.

[(4) The Secretary of State may by order amend subsection (1A) above by substituting a different sum for the sum for the time being specified there.]

Annual Return

S.48 – *Any registered charity whose income and expenditure exceeds £10,000 must within ten months of its financial year prepare and submit to the Commission an annual return in a form required by the Commission (Charities (Annual Return) Regulations 1998). These returns are provided to all registered charities by the commission and the information should be carefully checked before returning them to the commission.*

49 Offences

Any person who, without reasonable excuse, is persistently in default in relation to any requirement imposed—

(a) by section 45(3) [or (3A)] above (taken with section 45(4) or (5), as the case may require), or

(b) by section 47(2) or 48(2) above,

shall be guilty of an offence and liable on summary conviction to a fine not exceeding level 4 on the standard scale.

S.49 – *A criminal offence is committed by a trustee who persistently fails to produce an annual report and accounts or make them available for public inspection or produce annual returns to the Commission.*

PART VII

INCORPORATION OF CHARITY TRUSTEES

Part VII largely re-enacts the Charitable Trustees Incorporation Act 1872.

50 Incorporation of trustees of a charity

(1) Where—

    (a) the trustees of a charity, in accordance with section 52 below, apply to the Commissioners for a certificate of incorporation of the trustees as a body corporate, and

    (b) the Commissioners consider that the incorporation of the trustees would be in the interests of the charity,

the Commissioners may grant such a certificate, subject to such conditions or directions as they think fit to insert in it.

(2) The Commissioners shall not, however, grant such a certificate in a case where the charity appears to them to be required to be registered under section 3 above but is not so registered.

(3) On the grant of such a certificate—

    (a) the trustees of the charity shall become a body corporate by such name as is specified in the certificate; and

    (b) (without prejudice to the operation of section 54 below) any relevant rights or liabilities of those trustees shall become rights or liabilities of that body.

(4) After their incorporation the trustees—

    (a) may sue and be sued in their corporate name; and

    (b) shall have the same powers, and be subject to the same restrictions and limitations, as respects the holding, acquisition and disposal of property for or in connection with the purposes of the charity as they had or were subject to while unincorporated;

and any relevant legal proceedings that might have been continued or commenced by or against the trustees may be continued or commenced by or against them in their corporate name.

(5) A body incorporated under this section need not have a common seal.

(6) In this section—

    "relevant rights or liabilities" means rights or liabilities in connection with any property vesting in the body in question under section 51 below; and "relevant legal proceedings" means legal proceedings in connection with any such property.

> **S.50** – *Allows the Commission on request of the trustees to incorporate the trustees of a registered charity (but not strictly speaking the charity itself) and this corporate body may thereafter sue and be sued, hold assets and contract with third parties in their corporate name (e.g. "the Trustees of the X Charity" or "the X Charity Incorporated Trustees"). Under S.50(5) the incorporated trustees have the option of using a common seal – see S.60.*
>
> *Incorporation is very useful where a charity has a number of different properties, shares or other assets and its trustees are geographically widespread or change frequently, but see note to S.54 in relation to liability of trustees.*

51 Estate to vest in body corporate

The certificate of incorporation shall vest in the body corporate all real and personal estate, of whatever nature or tenure, belonging to or held by any person or persons in trust for the charity, and thereupon any person or persons in whose name or names any stocks, funds or securities are standing in trust for the charity, shall transfer them into the name of the body corporate, except that the foregoing provisions shall not apply to property vested in the official custodian.

> **S.51** – *This vests all property into the name of the corporate body immediately on incorporation except stocks and shares and other investments which would normally have to be transferred separately by the previous individual trustees.*

52 Applications for incorporation

(1) Every application to the Commissioners for a certificate of incorporation under this Part of this Act shall—

    (a) be in writing and signed by the trustees of the charity concerned; and

    (b) be accompanied by such documents or information as the Commissioners may require for the purpose of the application.

(2) The Commissioners may require—

    (a) any statement contained in any such application, or

    (b) any document or information supplied under subsection (1)(b) above,

to be verified in such manner as they may specify.

S.52 – *Provides for the method of application to the Commission for incorporation.*

53 Nomination of trustees, and filling up vacancies

(1) Before a certificate of incorporation is granted under this Part of this Act, trustees of the charity must have been effectually appointed to the satisfaction of the Commissioners.

(2) Where a certificate of incorporation is granted vacancies in the number of the trustees of the charity shall from time to time be filled up so far as required by the constitution or settlement of the charity, or by any conditions or directions in the certificate, by such legal means as would have been available for the appointment of new trustees of the charity if no certificate of incorporation had been granted, or otherwise as required by such conditions or directions.

S.53 – *Before they can be incorporated, the trustees must show the Commission that they have been effectually appointed. The Certificate of Incorporation does not change the existing method of appointment or retirement of trustees but, because the property of the charity is vested in the corporate body by virtue of S.51, there is usually no need for appointments of new trustees to be by deed once the trustees have been incorporated.*

Subject to the terms of the charity's governing instrument, a record of the appointment of a new trustee in the charity's minutes is generally sufficient.

54 Liability of trustees and others, notwithstanding incorporation

After a certificate of incorporation has been granted under this Part of this Act all trustees of the charity, notwithstanding their incorporation, shall be chargeable for such property as shall come into their hands, and shall be answerable and accountable for their own acts, receipts, neglects, and defaults, and for the due administration of the charity and its property, in the same manner and to the same extent as if no such incorporation had been effected.

S.54 – *Unlike incorporation as a charitable company, the trustees incorporated under Part VII of the Act obtain no protection from liability for claims in the event of a charity having insufficient money to meet those claims. In other words this form of incorporation is not appropriate if trustees wish to achieve the protection of limited liability.*

55 Certificate to be evidence of compliance with requirements for incorporation

A certificate of incorporation granted under this Part of this Act shall be conclusive evidence that all the preliminary requirements for incorporation under this Part of this Act have been complied with, and the date of incorporation mentioned in the certificate shall be deemed to be the date at which incorporation has taken place.

S.55 – *The Certificate of Incorporation is conclusive evidence of compliance and the date of incorporation is the date on the Certificate of Incorporation produced by the Commission.*

56 Power of Commissioners to amend certificate of incorporation

(1) The Commissioners may amend a certificate of incorporation either on the application of the incorporated body to which it relates or of their own motion.

(2) Before making any such amendment of their own motion, the Commissioners shall by notice in writing—

(a) inform the trustees of the relevant charity of their proposals, and
(b) invite those trustees to make representations to them within a time specified in the notice, being not less than one month from the date of the notice.

(3) The Commissioners shall take into consideration any representations made by those trustees within the time so specified, and may then (without further notice) proceed with their proposals either without modification or with such modifications as appear to them to be desirable.

(4) The Commissioners may amend a certificate of incorporation either—

(a) by making an order specifying the amendment; or
(b) by issuing a new certificate of incorporation taking account of the amendment.

S.56 – *This allows the Commission to amend the Certificate, either at the request of the incorporated trustees or off their own bat.*

57 Records of applications and certificates

(1) The Commissioners shall keep a record of all applications for, and certificates of, incorporation under this Part of this Act and shall preserve all documents sent to them under this Part of this Act.

(2) Any person may inspect such documents, under the direction of the Commissioners, and any person may require a copy or extract of any such document to be certified by a certificate signed by the secretary of the Commissioners.

S.57 – *The Commission must keep records of applications and certificates of incorporation available for public inspection.*

58 Enforcement of orders and directions

All conditions and directions inserted in any certificate of incorporation shall be binding upon and performed or observed by the trustees as trusts of the charity, and section 88 below shall apply to any trustee who fails to perform or observe any such condition or direction as it applies to a person guilty of disobedience to any such order of the Commissioners as is mentioned in that section.

S.58 – *All conditions contained in a Certificate of Incorporation have to be observed in the same way as trusts of the charity.*

59 Gifts to charity before incorporation to have same effect afterwards

After the incorporation of the trustees of any charity under this Part of this Act every donation, gift and disposition of property, real or personal, lawfully made before the incorporation but not having actually taken effect, or thereafter lawfully made, by deed, will or otherwise to or in favour of the charity, or the trustees of the charity, or otherwise for the purposes of the charity, shall take effect as if made to or in favour of the incorporated body or otherwise for the like purposes.

S.59 – *After incorporation, all gifts, donations or transfers to the charity, if not already implemented, will take effect as if made to the corporate body.*

60 Execution of documents by incorporated body

(1) This section has effect as respects the execution of documents by an incorporated body.

(2) If an incorporated body has a common seal, a document may be executed by the body by the affixing of its common seal.

(3) Whether or not it has a common seal, a document may be executed by an incorporated body either—

   (a) by being signed by a majority of the trustees of the relevant charity and expressed (in whatever form of words) to be executed by the body; or
   (b) by being executed in pursuance of an authority given under subsection (4) below.

(4) For the purposes of subsection (3)(b) above the trustees of the relevant charity in the case of an incorporated body may, subject to the trusts of the charity, confer on any two or more of their number—

   (a) a general authority, or
   (b) an authority limited in such manner as the trustees think fit,

to execute in the name and on behalf of the body documents for giving effect to transactions to which the body is a party.

(5) An authority under subsection (4) above—

   (a) shall suffice for any document if it is given in writing or by resolution of a meeting of the trustees of the relevant charity, notwithstanding the want of any formality that would be required in giving an authority apart from that subsection;
   (b) may be given so as to make the powers conferred exercisable by any of the trustees, or may be restricted to named persons or in any other way;
   (c) subject to any such restriction, and until it is revoked, shall, notwithstanding any change in the trustees of the relevant charity, have effect as a continuing authority given by the trustees from time to time of the charity and exercisable by such trustees.

(6) In any authority under subsection (4) above to execute a document in the name and on behalf of an incorporated body there shall, unless the contrary intention appears, be implied authority also to execute it for the body in the name and on behalf of the official custodian or of any other person, in any case in which the trustees could do so.

(7) A document duly executed by an incorporated body which makes it clear on its face that it is intended by the person or persons making it to be a deed has effect, upon delivery, as a deed; and it shall be presumed, unless a contrary intention is proved, to be delivered upon its being so executed.

(8) In favour of a purchaser a document shall be deemed to have been duly executed by such a body if it purports to be signed—

   (a) by a majority of the trustees of the relevant charity, or
   (b) by such of the trustees of the relevant charity as are authorised by the trustees of that charity to execute it in the name and on behalf of the body,

and, where the document makes it clear on its face that it is intended by the person or persons making it to be a deed, it shall be deemed to have been delivered upon its being executed.

For this purpose "purchaser" means a purchaser in good faith for valuable consideration and includes a lessee, mortgagee or other person who for valuable consideration acquires an interest in property.

> **S.60** – *Execution of documents by the incorporated trustees can be either :-*
>
> • *by the corporate body's common seal or*
>
> • *by the signatures of a majority of the trustees or*
>
> • *by signature of two or more trustees acting under written authority.*
>
> *The section also provides for the recording of any authority under Ss.60(4) & (5) and of a majority resolution – see S.60(8).*

61 Power of Commissioners to dissolve incorporated body

(1) Where the Commissioners are satisfied—

(a) that an incorporated body has no assets or does not operate, or

(b) that the relevant charity in the case of an incorporated body has ceased to exist, or

(c) that the institution previously constituting, or treated by them as constituting, any such charity has ceased to be, or (as the case may be) was not at the time of the body's incorporation, a charity, or

(d) that the purposes of the relevant charity in the case of an incorporated body have been achieved so far as is possible or are in practice incapable of being achieved,

they may of their own motion make an order dissolving the body as from such date as is specified in the order.

(2) Where the Commissioners are satisfied, on the application of the trustees of the relevant charity in the case of an incorporated body, that it would be in the interests of the charity for that body to be dissolved, the Commissioners may make an order dissolving the body as from such date as is specified in the order.

(3) Subject to subsection (4) below, an order made under this section with respect to an incorporated body shall have the effect of vesting in the trustees of the relevant charity, in trust for that charity, all property for the time being vested—

(a) in the body, or

(b) in any other person (apart from the official custodian), in trust for that charity.

(4) If the Commissioners so direct in the order—

    (a) all or any specified part of that property shall, instead of vesting in the trustees of the relevant charity, vest—

        (i) in a specified person as trustee for, or nominee of, that charity, or

        (ii) in such persons (other than the trustees of the relevant charity) as may be specified;

    (b) any specified investments, or any specified class or description of investments, held by any person in trust for the relevant charity shall be transferred—

        (i) to the trustees of that charity, or

        (ii) to any such person or persons as is or are mentioned in paragraph (a)(i) or (ii) above;

and for this purpose "specified" means specified by the Commissioners in the order.

(5) Where an order to which this subsection applies is made with respect to an incorporated body—

    (a) any rights or liabilities of the body shall become rights or liabilities of the trustees of the relevant charity; and

    (b) any legal proceedings that might have been continued or commenced by or against the body may be continued or commenced by or against those trustees.

(6) Subsection (5) above applies to any order under this section by virtue of which—

    (a) any property vested as mentioned in subsection (3) above is vested—

        (i) in the trustees of the relevant charity, or

        (ii) in any person as trustee for, or nominee of, that charity; or

    (b) any investments held by any person in trust for the relevant charity are required to be transferred—

        (i) to the trustees of that charity, or

        (ii) to any person as trustee for, or nominee of, that charity.

(7) Any order made by the Commissioners under this section may be varied or revoked by a further order so made.

S.61 – *The Commission may off its own bat dissolve a corporate body if for example the corporate body has no assets or does not operate or the charity has ceased to be a charity or its purposes have been achieved. In all other circumstances, dissolution of the corporate body can only take place on application by the trustees.*

S.61(3) – *Provides that an order dissolving the corporate body will vest the property in individual trustees unless the Commission otherwise order.*

S.61(7) – *Provides that any order under S.61 can be revoked or amended.*

62 Interpretation of Part VII

In this Part of this Act—

"incorporated body" means a body incorporated under section 50 above;

"the relevant charity", in relation to an incorporated body, means the charity the trustees of which have been incorporated as that body;

"the trustees", in relation to a charity, means the charity trustees.

S.62 – *Is an interpretation clause.*

PART VIII
CHARITABLE COMPANIES

63 Winding up

(1) Where a charity may be wound up by the High Court under the Insolvency Act 1986, a petition for it to be wound up under that Act by any court in England or Wales having jurisdiction may be presented by the Attorney General, as well as by any person authorised by that Act.

(2) Where a charity may be so wound up by the High Court, such a petition may also be presented by the Commissioners if, at any time after they have instituted an inquiry under section 8 above with respect to the charity, they are satisfied as mentioned in section 18(1)(a) or (b) above.

(3) Where a charitable company is dissolved, the Commissioners may make an application under section 651 of the Companies Act 1985 (power of court to declare dissolution of company void) for an order to be made under that section with respect to the company; and for this purpose subsection (1) of that section shall have effect in relation to a charitable company as if the reference to the liquidator of the company included a reference to the Commissioners.

(4) Where a charitable company's name has been struck off the register of companies under section 652 of the Companies Act 1985 (power of registrar to strike defunct company off register), the Commissioners may make an application under section 653(2) of that Act (objection to striking off by person aggrieved) for an order restoring the company's name to that register; and for this purpose section 653(2) shall have effect in relation to a charitable company as if the reference to any such person aggrieved as is there mentioned included a reference to the Commissioners.

(5) The powers exercisable by the Commissioners by virtue of this section shall be exercisable by them of their own motion, but shall be exercisable only with the agreement of the Attorney General on each occasion.

(6) In this section "charitable company" means a company which is a charity.

> **S.63** – *Although normally the Commission may exercise the same powers as the Attorney General in the taking of court proceedings see S.32(2), this does not apply to the presentation of a petition to wind up a charitable company - see S.32(2).*
>
> *However, under S.63(2) the Commission may present a winding up petition once they have issued a S.8 Inquiry and are satisfied either that there has been misconduct or mismanagement or that they need to act for the protection of the charity – see S.18(1).*
>
> *The Commission do have powers to apply to the Court to act for the protection of funds held by a charitable company (e.g. in S.63(3) for a declaration that a company dissolution is void) but under S.63(5) these powers and indeed all the powers contained in S.63 are exercisable only with the Attorney General's consent.*

64 Alteration of objects clause

(1) Where a charity is a company or other body corporate having power to alter the instruments establishing or regulating it as a body corporate, no exercise of that power which has the effect of the body ceasing to be a charity shall be valid so as to affect the application of—

    (a) any property acquired under any disposition or agreement previously made otherwise than for full consideration in money or money's worth, or any property representing property so acquired,

    (b) any property representing income which has accrued before the alteration is made, or

    (c) the income from any such property as aforesaid.

(2) Where a charity is a company, any alteration by it—

    (a) of the objects clause in its memorandum of association, or

    (b) of any other provision in its memorandum of association, or any provision in its articles of association, which is a provision directing or restricting the manner in which property of the company may be used or applied,

is ineffective without the prior written consent of the Commissioners.

(3) Where a company has made any such alteration in accordance with subsection (2) above and—

    (a) in connection with the alteration is required by virtue of—

        (i) section 6(1) of the Companies Act 1985 (delivery of documents following alteration of objects), or

(ii) that provision as applied by section 17(3) of that Act (alteration of condition in memorandum which could have been contained in articles), to deliver to the registrar of companies a printed copy of its memorandum, as altered, or

(b) is required by virtue of section 380(1) of that Act (registration etc of resolutions and agreements) to forward to the registrar a printed or other copy of the special resolution effecting the alteration,

the copy so delivered or forwarded by the company shall be accompanied by a copy of the Commissioner's consent.

(4) Section 6(3) of that Act (offences) shall apply to any default by a company in complying with subsection (3) above as it applies to any such default as is mentioned in that provision.

> **S.64** – *A charitable company cannot without consent of the Commission change its objects or any provision in its Memorandum and Articles of Association which restrict the use of its property and indeed any attempt to do so without consent would render the change invalid. For example, it cannot decide without such consent to give itself powers to remunerate the company's trustees/directors.*
>
> *This provision is policed by the requirement in S.64(3) that any resolution amending the Memorandum and Articles, which under the Companies Acts has to be delivered to the Registrar of Companies, is accompanied by a copy of the Commission's consent under S.64. Failure to do so is a criminal offence under S.6(3) Companies Act 1985.*

65 Invalidity of certain transactions

(1) Sections 35 and 35A of the Companies Act 1985 (capacity of company not limited by its memorandum; power of directors to bind company) do not apply to the acts of a company which is a charity except in favour of a person who—

(a) gives full consideration in money or money's worth in relation to the act in question, and

(b) does not know that the act is not permitted by the company's memorandum or, as the case may be, is beyond the powers of the directors,

or who does not know at the time the act is done that the company is a charity.

(2) However, where such a company purports to transfer or grant an interest in property, the fact that the act was not permitted by the company's memorandum or, as the case may be, that the directors in connection with the act exceeded any limitation on their powers under the company's constitution, does not affect the title of a person who subsequently acquires the property or any interest in it for full consideration without actual notice of any such circumstances affecting the validity of the company's act.

(3) In any proceedings arising out of subsection (1) above the burden of proving—

(a) that a person knew that an act was not permitted by the company's memorandum or was beyond the powers of the directors, or

(b) that a person knew that the company was a charity,

lies on the person making that allegation.

(4) Where a company is a charity, the ratification of an act under section 35(3) of the Companies Act 1985, or the ratification of a transaction to which section 322A of that Act applies (invalidity of certain transactions to which directors or their associates are parties), is ineffective without the prior written consent of the Commissioners.

S.65 – *While constitutionally certain transactions may be technically beyond the power of a company or its directors, they are nevertheless binding on a company under Sections 35 and 35(A) Companies Act 1985. However, under S.65(1) this rule only applies to a charitable company if the person who is wanting to enforce a contractual obligation against a charitable company was dealing with the company for value and did not know that it was a charitable company.*

Under S.65(2) a bona fide purchaser for value of charity property without notice of the fact that the company is exceeding its powers is also protected.

Under S.65(3) the burden of proof that someone dealing for value with a charitable company actually knew that the transaction was not permitted lies on the person alleging that that was the case.

Under S.65(4) ratification of certain transactions involving directors which would normally be permitted under the Companies Act 1985 will be in-effective without the prior written consent of the Commission.

66 Requirement of consent of Commissioners to certain acts

(1) Where a company is a charity—

(a) any approval given by the company for the purposes of any of the provisions of the Companies Act 1985 specified in subsection (2) below, and

(b) any affirmation by it for the purposes of section 322(2)(c) of that Act (affirmation of voidable arrangements under which assets are acquired by or from a director or person connected with him),

is ineffective without the prior written consent of the Commissioners.

(2) The provisions of the Companies Act 1985 referred to in subsection (1)(a) above are—

(a) section 312 (payment to director in respect of loss of office or retirement);

(b) section 313(1) (payment to director in respect of loss of office or retirement made in connection with transfer of undertaking or property of company);

(c) section 319(3) (incorporation in director's service contract of term whereby his employment will or may continue for a period of more than five years);

(d) section 320(1) (arrangement whereby assets are acquired by or from director or person connected with him);

(e) section 337(3)(a) (provision of funds to meet certain expenses incurred by director).

S.66 – *Certain acts (for instance providing benefits to trustees/directors) are invalid without Charity Commission consent. Such consent is unlikely to be forthcoming other than in exceptional circumstances.*

67 Name to appear on correspondence etc

Section 30(7) of the Companies Act 1985 (exemption from requirements relating to publication of name etc) shall not, in its application to any company which is a charity, have the effect of exempting the company from the requirements of section 349(1) of that Act (company's name to appear in its correspondence etc).

S.67 – *Notwithstanding exemptions allowed to non-charitable companies (S.30(7) Companies Act 1985) a charitable company must have its full name on correspondence, bills and so on.*

68 Status to appear on correspondence etc

(1) Where a company is a charity and its name does not include the word "charity" or the word "charitable" [then, subject to subsection (1A)], the fact that the company is a charity shall be stated . . . in legible characters—

(a) in all business letters of the company,

(b) in all its notices and other official publications,

(c) in all bills of exchange, promissory notes, endorsements, cheques and orders for money or goods purporting to be signed on behalf of the company,

(d) in all conveyances purporting to be executed by the company, and

(e) in all bills rendered by it and in all its invoices, receipts, and letters of credit.

[(1A) Where a company's name includes the word "elusen" or the word "elusennol" (the Welsh equivalents of the words "charity" and "charitable"), subsection (1) above shall not apply in relation to any document which is wholly in Welsh.

(1B) The statement required by subsection (1) above shall be in English, except that, in the case of a document which is otherwise wholly in Welsh, the statement may be in Welsh if it consists of or includes the word "elusen" or the word "elusennol".]

(2) In subsection (1)(d) above "conveyance" means any instrument creating, transferring, varying or extinguishing an interest in land.

(3) Subsections (2) to (4) of section 349 of the Companies Act 1985 (offences in connection with failure to include required particulars in business letters etc) shall apply in relation to a contravention of subsection (1) above, taking the reference in subsection (3)(b) of that section to a bill of parcels as a reference to any such bill as is mentioned in subsection (1)(e) above.

> **S.68** – *A company's charitable status must appear in legible English on all business letters, notices, invoices and deeds relating to land. This ties in with the requirements of S.5 in relation to most registered charities. In a wholly Welsh document the Welsh equivalent to "charity" or "charitable" may be used.*
>
> *Failure to comply is, as with S.5, a criminal offence.*

69 Investigation of accounts

(1) In the case of a charity which is a company the Commissioners may by order require that the condition and accounts of the charity for such period as they think fit shall be investigated and audited by an auditor appointed by them, being a person eligible for appointment as a company auditor under section 25 of the Companies Act 1989.

(2) An auditor acting under subsection (1) above—

(a) shall have a right of access to all books, accounts and documents relating to the charity which are in the possession or control of the charity trustees or to which the charity trustees have access;

(b) shall be entitled to require from any charity trustee, past or present, and from any past or present officer or employee of the charity such information and explanation as he thinks necessary for the performance of his duties;

(c) shall at the conclusion or during the progress of the audit make such reports to the Commissioners about the audit or about the accounts or affairs of the charity as he thinks the case requires, and shall send a copy of any such report to the charity trustees.

(3) The expenses of any audit under subsection (1) above, including the remuneration of the auditor, shall be paid by the Commissioners.

(4) If any person fails to afford an auditor any facility to which he is entitled under subsection (2) above the Commissioners may by order give to that person or to the charity trustees for the time being such directions as the Commissioners think appropriate for securing that the default is made good.

S.69 – The Commission is allowed by S.69(1) to appoint a professional auditor to investigate a charitable company's accounts and for that purpose the auditor may have access to books, documents and other information. His report to the Commission must be copied to the trustees/directors.

Unlike an audit required under S.43(6), the costs of an audit under S.69 lies with the Commission.

A person disobeying an order of the Commission under this section can be committed to prison for contempt – see S.88(c).

Part IX
Miscellaneous

Powers of investment

70 Relaxation of restrictions on wider-range investments

(1) The Secretary of State may by order made with the consent of the Treasury—

    (a) direct that, in the case of a trust fund consisting of property held by or in trust for a charity, any division of the fund in pursuance of section 2(1) of the Trustee Investments Act 1961 (trust funds to be divided so that wider-range and narrower-range investments are equal in value) shall be made so that the value of the wider-range part at the time of the division bears to the then value of the narrower-range part such proportion as is specified in the order;

    (b) provide that, in its application in relation to such a trust fund, that Act shall have effect subject to such modifications so specified as the Secretary of State considers appropriate in consequence of, or in connection with, any such direction.

(2) Where, before the coming into force of an order under this section, a trust fund consisting of property held by or in trust for a charity has already been divided in pursuance of section 2(1) of that Act, the fund may, notwithstanding anything in that provision, be again divided (once only) in pursuance of that provision during the continuance in force of the order.

(3) No order shall be made under this section unless a draft of the order has been laid before and approved by a resolution of each House of Parliament.

(4) Expressions used in this section which are also used in the Trustee Investments Act 1961 have the same meaning as in that Act.

(5) In the application of this section to Scotland, "charity" means a recognised body within the meaning of section 1(7) of the Law Reform (Miscellaneous Provisions) (Scotland) Act 1990.

S.70 – *Allows the Home Secretary with Treasury consent to alter in relation to charities only the effect of the Trustee Investments Act 1961 in relation to the division of trust funds where the governing document does not contain wider powers. The 1961 Act originally allowed trustees to invest not more than half of their capital in "wider range" securities, in other words in equities, while the remaining half or more had to be invested in narrower range securities such as gilt edged stock. The Charities (Trustee Investments Act 1961) Order 1995 allowed these proportions to be 75-25, though this has now been replaced by the Trustee Investments Act (Division of Trust Funds) Order 1996.*

At the date of publication legislation is impending (as the Trustee Bill) to repeal the Trustee Investments Act 1961 and to substitute a much less restrictive investment regime.

71 Extension of powers of investment

(1) The Secretary of State may by regulations made with the consent of the Treasury make, with respect to property held by or in trust for a charity, provision authorising a trustee to invest such property in any manner specified in the regulations, being a manner of investment not for the time being included in any Part of Schedule 1 to the Trustee Investments Act 1961.

(2) Regulations under this section may make such provision—

    (a) regulating the investment of property in any manner authorised by virtue of subsection (1) above, and

    (b) with respect to the variation and retention of investments so made,

as the Secretary of State considers appropriate.

(3) Such regulations may, in particular, make provision—

    (a) imposing restrictions with respect to the proportion of the property held by or in trust for a charity which may be invested in any manner authorised by virtue of subsection (1) above, being either restrictions applying to investment in any such manner generally or restrictions applying to investment in any particular such manner;

    (b) imposing the like requirements with respect to the obtaining and consideration of advice as are imposed by any of the provisions of section 6 of the Trustee

Investments Act 1961 (duty of trustees in choosing investments).

(4) Any power of investment conferred by any regulations under this section—

    (a) shall be in addition to, and not in derogation from, any power conferred otherwise than by such regulations; and

    (b) shall not be limited by the trusts of a charity (in so far as they are not contained in any Act or instrument made under an enactment) unless it is excluded by those trusts in express terms;

but any such power shall only be exercisable by a trustee in so far as a contrary intention is not expressed in any Act or in any instrument made under an enactment and relating to the powers of the trustee.

(5) No regulations shall be made under this section unless a draft of the regulations has been laid before and approved by a resolution of each House of Parliament.

(6) In this section "property"—

    (a) in England and Wales, means real or personal property of any description, including money and things in action, but does not include an interest in expectancy; and

    (b) in Scotland, means property of any description (whether heritable or moveable, corporeal or incorporeal) which is presently enjoyable, but does not include a future interest, whether vested or contingent;

and any reference to property held by or in trust for a charity is a reference to property so held, whether it is for the time being in a state of investment or not.

(7) In the application of this section to Scotland, "charity" means a recognised body within the meaning of section 1(7) of the Law Reform (Miscellaneous Provisions) (Scotland) Act 1990.

S.71 – *The Home Secretary can, again in relation only to charities and with Treasury consent, extend the breadth of wider range securities - see S.70 above. To date no regulations have been made under S.71.*

Government policy on the matter has moved on considerably since the 1992 legislation and the Law Commission recommended in its report "Trustee Powers and Duties" (Law Comm. No. 260) that trustees should have the same powers of investment as beneficial owners, provided that they obtained proper professional advice and considered the question of diversification of investments. Indeed the Treasury put forward proposals in 1996 which, had the 1997 General Election not intervened, would have given charity trustees all the powers of a beneficial owner provided that professional advice was obtained and investment portfolios were properly reviewed. If the Trustee Bill 2000 is given the Royal Assent in its present form the T.I.A. will be repealed and the investment regime suggested by the Law Commission will apply.

Disqualification for acting as charity trustee

72 Persons disqualified for being trustees of a charity

(1) Subject to the following provisions of this section, a person shall be disqualified for being a charity trustee or trustee for a charity if—

(a) he has been convicted of any offence involving dishonesty or deception;

(b) he has been adjudged bankrupt or sequestration of his estate has been awarded and (in either case) he has not been discharged;

(c) he has made a composition or arrangement with, or granted a trust deed for, his creditors and has not been discharged in respect of it;

(d) he has been removed from the office of charity trustee or trustee for a charity by an order made—

   (i) by the Commissioners under section 18(2)(i) above, or

   (ii) by the Commissioners under section 20(1A)(i) of the Charities Act 1960 (power to act for protection of charities) or under section 20(1)(i) of that Act (as in force before the commencement of section 8 of the Charities Act 1992), or

   (iii) by the High Court,

   on the grounds of any misconduct or mismanagement in the administration of the charity for which he was responsible or to which he was privy, or which he by his conduct contributed to or facilitated;

(e) he has been removed, under section 7 of the Law Reform (Miscellaneous Provisions) (Scotland) Act 1990 (powers of Court of Session to deal with management of charities), from being concerned in the management or control of any body;

(f) he is subject to a disqualification order under the Company Directors Disqualification Act 1986 or to an order made under section 429(2)(b) of the Insolvency Act 1986 (failure to pay under county court administration order).

(2) In subsection (1) above—

(a) paragraph (a) applies whether the conviction occurred before or after the commencement of that subsection, but does not apply in relation to any conviction which is a spent conviction for the purposes of the Rehabilitation of Offenders Act 1974;

(b) paragraph (b) applies whether the adjudication of bankruptcy or the sequestration occurred before or after the commencement of that subsection;

(c) paragraph (c) applies whether the composition or arrangement was made, or the trust deed was granted, before or after the commencement of that subsection; and

(d) paragraphs (d) to (f) apply in relation to orders made and removals effected before or after the commencement of that subsection.

(3) Where (apart from this subsection) a person is disqualified under subsection (1)(b) above for being a charity trustee or trustee for any charity which is a company, he

shall not be so disqualified if leave has been granted under section 11 of the Company Directors Disqualification Act 1986 (undischarged bankrupts) for him to act as director of the charity; and similarly a person shall not be disqualified under subsection (1)(f) above for being a charity trustee or trustee for such a charity if—

(a) in the case of a person subject to a disqualification order, leave under the order has been granted for him to act as director of the charity, or

(b) in the case of a person subject to an order under section 429(2)(b) of the Insolvency Act 1986, leave has been granted by the court which made the order for him to so act.

(4) The Commissioners may, on the application of any person disqualified under subsection (1) above, waive his disqualification either generally or in relation to a particular charity or a particular class of charities; but no such waiver may be granted in relation to any charity which is a company if—

(a) the person concerned is for the time being prohibited, by virtue of—
   (i) a disqualification order under the Company Directors Disqualification Act 1986, or
   (ii) section 11(1) or 12(2) of that Act (undischarged bankrupts; failure to pay under county court administration order),

   from acting as director of the charity; and

(b) leave has not been granted for him to act as director of any other company.

(5) Any waiver under subsection (4) above shall be notified in writing to the person concerned.

(6) For the purposes of this section the Commissioners shall keep, in such manner as they think fit, a register of all persons who have been removed from office as mentioned in subsection (1)(d) above either—

(a) by an order of the Commissioners made before or after the commencement of subsection (1) above, or

(b) by an order of the High Court made after the commencement of section 45(1) of the Charities Act 1992;

and, where any person is so removed from office by an order of the High Court, the court shall notify the Commissioners of his removal.

(7) The entries in the register kept under subsection (6) above shall be available for public inspection in legible form at all reasonable times.

S.72 – *Originally enacted in the 1992 Act to strengthen the powers of the Commission, this section disqualifies certain persons from becoming or remaining trustees in similar fashion to the disqualification of directors (cf Company Directors Disqualification Act 1976).*

Under S.72 a person is automatically disqualified from acting as a charity trustee if (amongst other things) he is:-

- convicted of an offence of dishonesty or deception (unless it is spent conviction under Rehabilitation of Offenders Act 1974).

- adjudged bankrupt or has made a composition with creditors and not discharged.

- removed from office by the Commission on grounds of misconduct or mismanagement of a charity

- disqualified from acting as a company director.

Under S.72(6) the Commission must keep a register of disqualified trustees.

73 Persons acting as charity trustee while disqualified

(1) Subject to subsection (2) below, any person who acts as a charity trustee or trustee for a charity while he is disqualified for being such a trustee by virtue of section 72 above shall be guilty of an offence and liable—

    (a) on summary conviction, to imprisonment for a term not exceeding six months or to a fine not exceeding the statutory maximum, or both;

    (b) on conviction on indictment, to imprisonment for a term not exceeding two years or to a fine, or both.

(2) Subsection (1) above shall not apply where—

    (a) the charity concerned is a company; and

    (b) the disqualified person is disqualified by virtue only of paragraph (b) or (f) of section 72(1) above.

(3) Any acts done as charity trustee or trustee for a charity by a person disqualified for being such a trustee by virtue of section 72 above shall not be invalid by reason only of that disqualification.

(4) Where the Commissioners are satisfied—

    (a) that any person has acted as charity trustee or trustee for a charity (other than an exempt charity) while disqualified for being such a trustee by virtue of section 72 above, and

    (b) that, while so acting, he has received from the charity any sums by way of remuneration or expenses, or any benefit in kind, in connection with his acting as charity trustee or trustee for the charity,

they may by order direct him to repay to the charity the whole or part of any such sums, or (as the case may be) to pay to the charity the whole or part of the monetary value (as determined by them) of any such benefit.

(5) Subsection (4) above does not apply to any sums received by way of remuneration or expenses in respect of any time when the person concerned was not disqualified for being a charity trustee or trustee for the charity.

S.73 – *It is a criminal offence to act as a trustee while disqualified. However, under S.73(3)(a) the acts of a disqualified trustee do not invalidate the decision making of the trustees. Action against a disqualified trustee requires the consent of the Director of Public Prosecutions – see S.94.*

Small charities

S.74 and S.75 – Small Charities.
While normally cy-près schemes under S.13 of the Act are used by the Commission to effect changes to allow capital or income to be used for other similar purposes, the comprehensive pre-requisites and procedures for cy-près schemes can be avoided if the charity is small and holds no land for special purposes. The Home Secretary can by order raise the Sections 74 and 75 limits, but has not yet chosen to do so.

Sections 74 and 75 do not apply to exempt charities or to charitable companies.

74 Power to transfer all property, modify objects etc

(1) This section applies to a charity if—

   (a) its gross income in its last financial year did not exceed £5,000, and
   (b) it does not hold any land on trusts which stipulate that the land is to be used for the purposes, or any particular purposes, of the charity,

and it is neither an exempt charity nor a charitable company.

(2) Subject to the following provisions of this section, the charity trustees of a charity to which this section applies may resolve for the purposes of this section—

   (a) that all the property of the charity should be transferred to such other charity as is specified in the resolution, being either a registered charity or a charity which is not required to be registered;
   (b) that all the property of the charity should be divided, in such manner as is specified in the resolution, between such two or more other charities as are so specified, being in each case either a registered charity or a charity which is not required to be registered;

   (c) that the trusts of the charity should be modified by replacing all or any of the purposes of the charity with such other purposes, being in law charitable, as are specified in the resolution;

   (d) that any provision of the trusts of the charity—

      (i) relating to any of the powers exercisable by the charity trustees in the administration of the charity, or

      (ii) regulating the procedure to be followed in any respect in connection with its administration,

should be modified in such manner as is specified in the resolution.

(3) Any resolution passed under subsection (2) above must be passed by a majority of not less than two-thirds of such charity trustees as vote on the resolution.

(4) The charity trustees of a charity to which this section applies ("the transferor charity") shall not have power to pass a resolution under subsection (2)(a) or (b) above unless they are satisfied—

   (a) that the existing purposes of the transferor charity have ceased to be conducive to a suitable and effective application of the charity's resources; and

   (b) that the purposes of the charity or charities specified in the resolution are as similar in character to the purposes of the transferor charity as is reasonably practicable;

and before passing the resolution they must have received from the charity trustees of the charity, or (as the case may be) of each of the charities, specified in the resolution written confirmation that those trustees are willing to accept a transfer of property under this section.

(5) The charity trustees of any such charity shall not have power to pass a resolution under subsection (2)(c) above unless they are satisfied—

   (a) that the existing purposes of the charity (or, as the case may be, such of them as it is proposed to replace) have ceased to be conducive to a suitable and effective application of the charity's resources; and

   (b) that the purposes specified in the resolution are as similar in character to those existing purposes as is practical in the circumstances.

(6) Where charity trustees have passed a resolution under subsection (2) above, they shall—

   (a) give public notice of the resolution in such manner as they think reasonable in the circumstances; and

   (b) send a copy of the resolution to the Commissioners, together with a statement of their reasons for passing it.

(7) The Commissioners may, when considering the resolution, require the charity trustees to provide additional information or explanation—

   (a) as to the circumstances in and by reference to which they have determined to act under this section, or

(b) relating to their compliance with this section in connection with the resolution;

and the Commissioners shall take into account any representations made to them by persons appearing to them to be interested in the charity where those representations are made within the period of six weeks beginning with the date when the Commissioners receive a copy of the resolution by virtue of subsection (6)(b) above.

(8) Where the Commissioners have so received a copy of a resolution from any charity trustees and it appears to them that the trustees have complied with this section in connection with the resolution, the Commissioners shall, within the period of three months beginning with the date when they receive the copy of the resolution, notify the trustees in writing either—

(a) that the Commissioners concur with the resolution; or
(b) that they do not concur with it.

(9) Where the Commissioners so notify their concurrence with the resolution, then—

(a) if the resolution was passed under subsection (2)(a) or (b) above, the charity trustees shall arrange for all the property of the transferor charity to be transferred in accordance with the resolution and on terms that any property so transferred—
   (i) shall be held and applied by the charity to which it is transferred ("the transferee charity") for the purposes of that charity, but
   (ii) shall, as property of the transferee charity, nevertheless be subject to any restrictions on expenditure to which it is subject as property of the transferor charity,

   and those trustees shall arrange for it to be so transferred by such date as may be specified in the notification; and

(b) if the resolution was passed under subsection (2)(c) or (d) above, the trusts of the charity shall be deemed, as from such date as may be specified in the notification, to have been modified in accordance with the terms of the resolution.

(10) For the purpose of enabling any property to be transferred to a charity under this section, the Commissioners shall have power, at the request of the charity trustees of that charity, to make orders vesting any property of the transferor charity—

(a) in the charity trustees of the first-mentioned charity or in any trustee for that charity, or
(b) in any other person nominated by those charity trustees to hold the property in trust for that charity.

(11) The Secretary of State may by order amend subsection (1) above by substituting a different sum for the sum for the time being specified there.

(12) In this section—

(a) "charitable company" means a charity which is a company or other body corporate; and

(b) references to the transfer of property to a charity are references to its transfer—

  (i) to the charity trustees, or

  (ii) to any trustee for the charity, or

  (iii) to a person nominated by the charity trustees to hold it in trust for the charity,

as the charity trustees may determine.

S.74 – *Small charities having a gross income of under £5,000 may agree (by a two thirds majority of trustees) to pass their capital to one or more other charities or to alter the charity's objects or administrative procedures provided that the trustees are satisfied that its funds cannot effectively be used by the recipient charity. There is no reference in S.74 to the spirit of the original gift or to the intentions of those who set up the charity in the first place; all that is required is that the purposes of the charity have ceased to be helpful in enabling proper use of the charity's resources and that the recipient charity has objects which are as similar in character to the purposes of the original charity as is reasonably practicable. Once the resolution has been passed, it is copied to the Commission who must tell the trustees within three months whether or not they concur with the transfer.*

Although any restrictions on spending capital still apply to the property transferred, it is possible that they can be dealt with under the power to spend capital contained in S.75.

75 Power to spend capital

(1) This section applies to a charity if—

  (a) it has a permanent endowment which does not consist of or comprise any land, and

  (b) its gross income in its last financial year did not exceed £1,000,

and it is neither an exempt charity nor a charitable company.

(2) Where the charity trustees of a charity to which this section applies are of the opinion that the property of the charity is too small, in relation to its purposes, for any useful purpose to be achieved by the expenditure of income alone, they may resolve for the purposes of this section that the charity ought to be freed from the restrictions with respect to expenditure of capital to which its permanent endowment is subject.

(3) Any resolution passed under subsection (2) above must be passed by a majority of not less than two-thirds of such charity trustees as vote on the resolution.

(4) Before passing such a resolution the charity trustees must consider whether any reasonable possibility exists of effecting a transfer or division of all the charity's property under section 74 above (disregarding any such transfer or division as would, in their opinion, impose on the charity an unacceptable burden of costs).

(5) Where charity trustees have passed a resolution under subsection (2) above, they shall—

(a) give public notice of the resolution in such manner as they think reasonable in the circumstances; and

(b) send a copy of the resolution to the Commissioners, together with a statement of their reasons for passing it.

(6) The Commissioners may, when considering the resolution, require the charity trustees to provide additional information or explanation—

(a) as to the circumstances in and by reference to which they have determined to act under this section, or

(b) relating to their compliance with this section in connection with the resolution;

and the Commissioners shall take into account any representations made to them by persons appearing to them to be interested in the charity where those representations are made within the period of six weeks beginning with the date when the Commissioners receive a copy of the resolution by virtue of subsection (5)(b) above.

(7) Where the Commissioners have so received a copy of a resolution from any charity trustees and it appears to them that the trustees have complied with this section in connection with the resolution, the Commissioners shall, within the period of three months beginning with the date when they receive the copy of the resolution, notify the trustees in writing either—

(a) that the Commissioners concur with the resolution; or

(b) that they do not concur with it.

(8) Where the Commissioners so notify their concurrence with the resolution, the charity trustees shall have, as from such date as may be specified in the notification, power by virtue of this section to expend any property of the charity without regard to any such restrictions as are mentioned in subsection (2) above.

(9) The Secretary of State may by order amend subsection (1) above by substituting a different sum for the sum for the time being specified there.

(10) In this section "charitable company" means a charity which is a company or other body corporate.

S.75 – *Allows permanent endowment (capital which the governing document does not allow to be spent) to be used. In this case the gross income of the charity must be under £1,000 and its permanent endowment must not comprise any land. As with the S.74 procedure a two thirds majority of the trustees must vote on the resolution on the basis that they consider that the property of the charity is too small in relation to its purposes to achieve any useful purpose by the expenditure of income alone.*

In appropriate cases it might be sensible to use the S.75 procedure first, thus freeing the charity of the permanent endowment restriction, and then to transfer the funds to the recipient charity under S.74.

Local charities

76 Local authority's index of local charities

(1) The council of a county [or county borough] or of a district or London borough and the Common Council of the City of London may maintain an index of local charities or of any class of local charities in the council's area, and may publish information contained in the index, or summaries or extracts taken from it.

(2) A council proposing to establish or maintaining under this section an index of local charities or of any class of local charities shall, on request, be supplied by the Commissioners free of charge with copies of such entries in the register of charities as are relevant to the index or with particulars of any changes in the entries of which copies have been supplied before; and the Commissioners may arrange that they will without further request supply a council with particulars of any such changes.

(3) An index maintained under this section shall be open to public inspection at all reasonable times.

(4) A council may employ any voluntary organisation as their agent for the purposes of this section, on such terms and within such limits (if any) or in such cases as they may agree; and for this purpose "voluntary organisation" means any body of which the activities are carried on otherwise than for profit, not being a public or local authority.

(5) A joint board discharging any of a council's functions shall have the same powers under this section as the council as respects local charities in the council's area which are established for purposes similar or complementary to any services provided by the board.

S.76 – *A local authority can with Commission help maintain an index of local charities which will be open to inspection. However, since the opening of the Charity Commission Website, the Commission no longer issues local authorities with reports about local charities.*

77 Reviews of local charities by local authority

(1) The council of a county [or county borough] or of a district or London borough and the Common Council of the City of London may, subject to the following provisions of this section, initiate, and carry out in co-operation with the charity trustees, a review of the working of any group of local charities with the same or similar purposes in the council's area, and may make to the Commissioners such report on the review and such recommendations arising from it as the council after consultation with the trustees think fit.

(2) A council having power to initiate reviews under this section may co-operate with other persons in any review by them of the working of local charities in the council's area (with or without other charities), or may join with other persons in initiating and carrying out such a review.

(3) No review initiated by a council under this section shall extend to any charity without the consent of the charity trustees, nor to any ecclesiastical charity.

(4) No review initiated under this section by the council of a district shall extend to the working in any county of a local charity established for purposes similar or complementary to any services provided by county councils unless the review so extends with the consent of the council of that county.

[(4A) Subsection (4) above does not apply in relation to Wales.]

(5) Subsections (4) and (5) of section 76 above shall apply for the purposes of this section as they apply for the purposes of that section.

S.77 – *Local authorities can review local charities in their area and make reports and recommendations to the Commission.*

78 Co-operation between charities, and between charities and local authorities

(1) Any local council and any joint board discharging any functions of such a council—

(a) may make, with any charity established for purposes similar or complementary to services provided by the council or board, arrangements for co-ordinating the activities of the council or board and those of the charity in the interests of persons who may benefit from those services or from the charity; and

(b) shall be at liberty to disclose to any such charity in the interests of those persons any information obtained in connection with the services provided by the council or board, whether or not arrangements have been made with the charity under this subsection.

In this subsection "local council" means[, in relation to England,] the council of a county, or of a district, London borough, [or parish], and includes also the Common Council of the City of London and the Council of the Isles of Scilly [and, in relation to Wales, the council of a county, county borough or community].

(2) Charity trustees shall, notwithstanding anything in the trusts of the charity, have power by virtue of this subsection to do all or any of the following things, where it appears to them likely to promote or make more effective the work of the charity, and may defray the expense of so doing out of any income or money applicable as income of the charity, that is to say—

(a) they may co-operate in any review undertaken under section 77 above or otherwise of the working of charities or any class of charities;

(b) they may make arrangements with an authority acting under subsection (1) above or with another charity for co-ordinating their activities and those of the authority or of the other charity;

(c) they may publish information of other charities with a view to bringing them to the notice of those for whose benefit they are intended.

> **S.78** – *Local authorities and local charities can co-operate with each other in the interests of local beneficiaries, for example in the provision of housing or of services to the poor.*

79 Parochial charities

(1) Where trustees hold any property for the purposes of a public recreation ground, or of allotments (whether under inclosure Acts or otherwise), for the benefit of inhabitants of a parish having a parish council, or for other charitable purposes connected with such a parish, except for an ecclesiastical charity, they may with the approval of the Commissioners and with the consent of the parish council transfer the property to the parish council or to persons appointed by the parish council; and the council or their appointees shall hold the property on the same trusts and subject to the same conditions as the trustees did.

This subsection shall apply to property held for any public purposes as it applies to property held for charitable purposes.

(2) Where the charity trustees of a parochial charity in a parish, not being an ecclesiastical charity nor a charity founded within the preceding forty years, do not include persons elected by the local government electors, ratepayers or inhabitants of the parish or appointed by the parish council or parish meeting, the parish council or parish meeting may appoint additional charity trustees, to such number as the Commissioners may allow; and if there is a sole charity trustee not elected or appointed as aforesaid of any such charity, the number of the charity trustees may, with the approval of the Commissioners, be increased to three of whom one may be nominated by the person holding the office of the sole trustee and one by the parish council or parish meeting.

(3) Where, under the trusts of a charity other than an ecclesiastical charity, the inhabitants of a rural parish (whether in vestry or not) or a select vestry were formerly (in 1894) entitled to appoint charity trustees for, or trustees or beneficiaries of, the charity, then—

(a) in a parish having a parish council, the appointment shall be made by the parish council or, in the case of beneficiaries, by persons appointed by the parish council; and

(b) in a parish not having a parish council, the appointment shall be made by the parish meeting.

(4) Where overseers as such or, except in the case of an ecclesiastical charity, churchwardens as such were formerly (in 1894) charity trustees of or trustees for a parochial charity in a rural parish, either alone or jointly with other persons, then instead of the former overseer or church warden trustees there shall be trustees (to a number not greater than that of the former overseer or churchwarden trustees) appointed by the parish council or, if there is no parish council, by the parish meeting.

(5) Where, outside Greater London (other than the outer London boroughs), overseers of a parish as such were formerly (in 1927) charity trustees of or trustees for any charity, either alone or jointly with other persons, then instead of the former overseer trustees there shall be trustees (to a number not greater than that of the former overseer trustees) appointed by the parish council or, if there is no parish council, by the parish meeting.

(6) In the case of an urban parish existing immediately before the passing of the Local Government Act 1972 which after 1st April 1974 is not comprised in a parish, the power of appointment under subsection (5) above shall be exercisable by the district council.

(7) In the application of the foregoing provisions of this section to Wales—

(a) for references in subsections (1) and (2) to a parish or a parish council there shall be substituted respectively references to a community or a community council;

(b) for references in subsections (3)(a) and (b) to a parish, a parish council or a parish meeting there shall be substituted respectively references to a community, a community council or the [council of the county or (as the case may be) county borough];

(c) for references in subsections (4) and (5) to a parish council or a parish meeting there shall be substituted respectively references to a community council or the [council of the county or (as the case may be) county borough].

(8) Any appointment of a charity trustee or trustee for a charity which is made by virtue of this section shall be for a term of four years, and a retiring trustee shall be eligible for re-appointment but—

(a) on an appointment under subsection (2) above, where no previous appointments have been made by virtue of that subsection or of the corresponding provision of the Local Government Act 1894 or the Charities Act 1960, and more than one trustee is appointed, half of those appointed (or as nearly as may be) shall be appointed for a term of two years; and

(b) an appointment made to fill a casual vacancy shall be for the remainder of the term of the previous appointment.

[(9) This section shall not affect the trusteeship, control or management of any [foundation or voluntary school within the meaning of the School Standards and Framework Act 1998.]]

(10) The provisions of this section shall not extend to the Isles of Scilly, and shall have effect subject to any order (including any future order) made under any enactment relating to local government with respect to local government areas or the powers of local authorities.

(11) In this section the expression "formerly (in 1894)" relates to the period immediately before the passing of the Local Government Act 1894, and the expression "formerly (in 1927)" to the period immediately before 1st April 1927; and the word "former" shall be construed accordingly.

> **S.79** – *This provision, for the trusteeship and running of public recreation grounds or allotments by parish councils, re-enacts 19th century statutory provisions relating to the establishment of parish councils (in England) and community councils (in Wales), though the provisions do not apply to ecclesiastical charities nor to foundation or voluntary aided schools. S.79 applies only to land which is held on charitable trusts, not simply subject to covenants to be used only as a recreation ground.*
>
> *Whether parish councils or indeed any other local authority should in fact be trustees of local charities, given the inevitable confusion between politics and trustee responsibilities, is open to doubt and trustees and local authorities to whom this section applies should discuss the matter with the Commission.*

Scottish charities

80 Supervision by Commissioners of certain Scottish charities

(1) The following provisions of this Act, namely—

    (a) sections 8 and 9,

    (b) section 18 (except subsection (2)(ii)), and

    (c) section 19,

shall have effect in relation to any recognised body which is managed or controlled wholly or mainly in or from England or Wales as they have effect in relation to a charity.

(2) Where—

    (a) a recognised body is managed or controlled wholly or mainly in or from Scotland, but

    (b) any person in England and Wales holds any property on behalf of the body or of any person concerned in its management or control,

then, if the Commissioners are satisfied as to the matters mentioned in subsection (3) below, they may make an order requiring the person holding the property not to part with it without their approval.

(3) The matters referred to in subsection (2) above are—

    (a) that there has been any misconduct or mismanagement in the administration of the body; and

    (b) that it is necessary or desirable to make an order under that subsection for the purpose of protecting the property of the body or securing a proper application of such property for the purposes of the body;

and the reference in that subsection to the Commissioners being satisfied as to those matters is a reference to their being so satisfied on the basis of such information as may be supplied to them by the [Secretary of State].

(4) Where—

    (a) any person in England and Wales holds any property on behalf of a recognised body or of any person concerned in the management or control of such a body, and

    (b) the Commissioners are satisfied (whether on the basis of such information as may be supplied to them by the [Secretary of State] or otherwise)—

        (i) that there has been any misconduct or mismanagement in the administration of the body, and

        (ii) that it is necessary or desirable to make an order under this subsection for the purpose of protecting the property of the body or securing a proper application of such property for the purposes of the body, the Commissioners may by order vest the property in such recognised body or charity as is specified in the order in accordance with subsection (5) below, or require any persons in whom the property is vested to transfer it to any such body or charity, or appoint any person to transfer the property to any such body or charity.

(5) The Commissioners may specify in an order under subsection (4) above such other recognised body or such charity as they consider appropriate, being a body or charity whose purposes are, in the opinion of the Commissioners, as similar in character to those of the body referred to in paragraph (a) of that subsection as is reasonably practicable; but the Commissioners shall not so specify any body or charity unless they have received—

(a) from the persons concerned in the management or control of the body, or
(b) from the charity trustees of the charity,

as the case may be, written confirmation that they are willing to accept the property.

(6) In this section "recognised body" has the same meaning as in Part I of the Law Reform (Miscellaneous Provisions) (Scotland) Act 1990 (Scottish charities).

S.80 – *At present there is no precise equivalent in Scotland to the Commission and there is no registration of charities, although bodies recognised as being entitled to tax relief under S.505 Income and Corporation Taxes Act 1988 are subject to supervision of the Lord Advocate and the Court of Session. Indeed, the Lord Advocate has similar investigative powers to the Charity Commission.*

In consequence, the Commission have supervisory powers over recognised Scottish charities which are controlled from England or Wales or where a person in England and Wales holds property on trust for the recognised body although it is controlled from Scotland. The supervisory powers are similar to Sections 8/9 (enquiries/calling for documents) and to Sections 18/19 (Commission's protective powers) but there is no jurisdiction to make schemes for recognised Scottish charities.

Administrative provisions about charities

81 Manner of giving notice of charity meetings, etc

(1) All notices which are required or authorised by the trusts of a charity to be given to a charity trustee, member or subscriber may be sent by post, and, if sent by post, may be addressed to any address given as his in the list of charity trustees, members or subscribers for the time being in use at the office or principal office of the charity.

(2) Where any such notice required to be given as aforesaid is given by post, it shall be deemed to have been given by the time at which the letter containing it would be delivered in the ordinary course of post.

(3) No notice required to be given as aforesaid of any meeting or election need be given to any charity trustee, member or subscriber, if in the list above mentioned he has no address in the United Kingdom.

S.81 – *Provides for the service of notices to trustees, members and others entitled in the charity's governing document to attend charity meetings. In theory, the section only requires service of notices within the UK, though in practice it would be sensible to send notices to all who are entitled to attend given the comparative simplicity of worldwide communications. Notices are deemed to be delivered in the ordinary course of post.*

82 Manner of executing instruments

(1) Charity trustees may, subject to the trusts of the charity, confer on any of their body (not being less than two in number) a general authority, or an authority limited in such manner as the trustees think fit, to execute in the names and on behalf of the trustees assurances or other deeds or instruments for giving effect to transactions to which the trustees are a party; and any deed or instrument executed in pursuance of an authority so given shall be of the same effect as if executed by the whole body.

(2) An authority under subsection (1) above—

   (a) shall suffice for any deed or instrument if it is given in writing or by resolution of a meeting of the trustees, notwithstanding the want of any formality that would be required in giving an authority apart from that subsection;

   (b) may be given so as to make the powers conferred exercisable by any of the trustees, or may be restricted to named persons or in any other way;

   (c) subject to any such restriction, and until it is revoked, shall, notwithstanding any change in the charity trustees, have effect as a continuing authority given by the charity trustees from time to time of the charity and exercisable by such trustees.

(3) In any authority under this section to execute a deed or instrument in the names and on behalf of charity trustees there shall, unless the contrary intention appears, be implied authority also to execute it for them in the name and on behalf of the official custodian or of any other person, in any case in which the charity trustees could do so.

(4) Where a deed or instrument purports to be executed in pursuance of this section, then in favour of a person who (then or afterwards) in good faith acquires for money or money's worth an interest in or charge on property or the benefit of any covenant or agreement expressed to be entered into by the charity trustees, it shall be conclusively presumed to have been duly executed by virtue of this section.

(5) The powers conferred by this section shall be in addition to and not in derogation of any other powers.

S.82 – *The general rule of law is that trustees must act personally and cannot delegate their decision-making unless the governing instrument or some statutory provision so allows; even then a trustee cannot abrogate his responsibilities as a trustee.*

Clearly, in a charity of any size, a trustee will not be able to assimilate all details and trustees have long been permitted by S.25 Trustee Act 1925 to employ staff and agents or organise volunteers to carry out the charity's activities. In doing so, the trustees do not throw away their responsibilities. Indeed the employee, volunteer or agent acts in accordance with the policies laid down by the trustees and regular reports should always be made to the trustees showing how their policies are being implemented.

S.82 provides authority for at least two trustees to sign and seal documents (including cheques) either under a written authority or by resolution of a meeting of trustees. In the usual way the purchaser for value acting in good faith is protected in the event of there being some invalidity in the authority.

83 Transfer and evidence of title to property vested in trustees

(1) Where, under the trusts of a charity, trustees of property held for the purposes of the charity may be appointed or discharged by resolution of a meeting of the charity trustees, members or other persons, a memorandum declaring a trustee to have been so appointed or discharged shall be sufficient evidence of that fact if the memorandum is signed either at the meeting by the person presiding or in some other manner directed by the meeting and is attested by two persons present at the meeting.

(2) A memorandum evidencing the appointment or discharge of a trustee under subsection (1) above, if executed as a deed, shall have the like operation under section 40 of the Trustee Act 1925 (which relates to vesting declarations as respects trust property in deeds appointing or discharging trustees) as if the appointment or discharge were effected by the deed.

(3) For the purposes of this section, where a document purports to have been signed and attested as mentioned in subsection (1) above, then on proof (whether by

evidence or as a matter of presumption) of the signature the document shall be presumed to have been so signed and attested, unless the contrary is shown.

(4) This section shall apply to a memorandum made at any time, except that subsection (2) shall apply only to those made after the commencement of the Charities Act 1960.

(5) This section shall apply in relation to any institution to which the Literary and Scientific Institutions Act 1854 applies as it applies in relation to a charity.

S.83 – *Contains provisions evidencing the appointment or discharge of trustees, except where the governing document contains an alternative procedure.*

A memorandum signed by the person chairing the meeting of trustees at which the resolution was made and witnessed by two other trustees attending that meeting is sufficient.

If the charity owns property, it is wise for any such memorandum or other document appointing the new trustees to be by deed because under S.40 Trustee Act 1925 land belonging to the trust is automatically vested in the newly appointed trustees. A charity should obtain legal advice if land has to be transferred on an appointment of new trustees, given that most land in England and Wales is registered in HM Land Registry.

PART X

SUPPLEMENTARY

84 Supply by Commissioners of copies of documents open to public inspection

The Commissioners shall, at the request of any person, furnish him with copies of, or extracts from, any document in their possession which is for the time being open to inspection under Parts II to VI of this Act.

S.84 – *The Commission must provide copies of documents which are open to inspection under Parts II to VI. This includes the register (which is available on the Commission's Website – see the Introduction) and annual reports and accounts of particular charities.*

---

85 Fees and other amounts payable to Commissioners

(1) The Secretary of State may by regulations require the payment to the Commissioners of such fees as may be prescribed by the regulations in respect of—

(a) the discharge by the Commissioners of such functions under the enactments relating to charities as may be so prescribed;

(b) the inspection of the register of charities or of other material kept by them under those enactments, or the furnishing of copies of or extracts from documents so kept.

(2) Regulations under this section may—

(a) confer, or provide for the conferring of, exemptions from liability to pay a prescribed fee;

(b) provide for the remission or refunding of a prescribed fee (in whole or in part) in circumstances prescribed by the regulations.

(3) Any regulations under this section which require the payment of a fee in respect of any matter for which no fee was previously payable shall not be made unless a draft of the regulations has been laid before and approved by a resolution of each House of Parliament.

(4) The Commissioners may impose charges of such amounts as they consider reasonable in respect of the supply of any publications produced by them.

(5) Any fees and other payments received by the Commissioners by virtue of this section shall be paid into the Consolidated Fund.

S.85 – *The Home Secretary is entitled to make regulations as to the charging of fees by the Commission and has in fact done so but effectively only in relation to provision of copy documents and certain publications – see the Charity Commissioners' Fees (Copies and Extracts) Regulations 1992 (SI.2986). However, a positive resolution of both Houses of Parliament is required because the question of the Commission charging for its services, which it has never yet done, is a matter for public debate. Furthermore, any charges may go to the Consolidated Fund rather than to the Commission itself, so would be in the nature of indirect taxation.*

86 Regulations and orders

(1) Any regulations or order of the Secretary of State under this Act—

(a) shall be made by statutory instrument; and

(b) (subject to subsection (2) below) shall be subject to annulment in pursuance of a resolution of either House of Parliament.

(2) Subsection (1)(b) above does not apply—

(a) to an order under section 17(2), 70 or 99(2);

(b) to any regulations under section 71; or

(c) to any regulations to which section 85(3) applies.

(3) Any regulations of the Secretary of State or the Commissioners and any order of the Secretary of State under this Act may make—

(a) different provision for different cases; and

(b) such supplemental, incidental, consequential or transitional provision or savings as the Secretary of State or, as the case may be, the Commissioners consider appropriate.

(4) Before making any regulations under section 42, 44 or 45 above the Secretary of State shall consult such persons or bodies of persons as he considers appropriate.

S.86 – *The Home Secretary may make regulations and orders under the Act and these are generally subject to negative resolution of Parliament which means that either House of Parliament is able to annul an order which has been laid before it. However, certain orders require a positive resolution of both Houses on the grounds that they could be more controversial; these include:*

- *changes to charities governed by public general acts (S.17),*

- *changes to restrictions, and extension of investment powers under, the Trustee Investments Act 1961 (S.71) and*

- *fee regulations (S.85).*

S.86(4) – *Regulations made in relation to Charity Reports and Accounts also require prior consultation, (e.g. with the accountancy and other professions).*

---

87 Enforcement of requirements by order of Commissioners

(1) If a person fails to comply with any requirement imposed by or under this Act then (subject to subsection (2) below) the Commissioners may by order give him such directions as they consider appropriate for securing that the default is made good.

(2) Subsection (1) above does not apply to any such requirement if—

(a) a person who fails to comply with, or is persistently in default in relation to, the requirement is liable to any criminal penalty; or

(b) the requirement is imposed—

(i) by an order of the Commissioners to which section 88 below applies, or

(ii) by a direction of the Commissioners to which that section applies by virtue of section 90(2) below.

S.87 – *To reinforce the Commission's monitoring and supervisory role and to enforce compliance, the Commission can direct a trustee or some other person to repay money to a charity or in some other way make good a default. However, see S.88 in relation to criminal liabilities.*

88 Enforcement of orders of Commissioners

A person guilty of disobedience—

(a) to an order of the Commissioners under section 9(1), 44(2), 61, 73 or 80 above; or

(b) to an order of the Commissioners under section 16 or 18 above requiring a transfer of property or payment to be called for or made; or

(c) to an order of the Commissioners requiring a default under this Act to be made good;

may on the application of the Commissioners to the High Court be dealt with as for disobedience to an order of the High Court.

S.88 – *The Commission can apply to the High Court for committal of a person to prison in the same way as for disobedience to a High Court order. This relates to default under:*

- *S.9(1) (production of documents and information)*

- *Ss. 16 and 18 (requiring transfers of property or payments to be made)*

- *S.44 (provision of facilities for audit of a charity)*

- *S.58 (directions and conditions in a certificate of incorporation)*

- *S.61 (dissolution of a corporate body)*

- *S.73 (orders for repayment by a disqualified trustee)*

- *S.80 (orders or directions relating to Scottish charities)*

89 Other provisions as to orders of Commissioners

(1) Any order made by the Commissioners under this Act may include such incidental or supplementary provisions as the Commissioners think expedient for carrying into effect the objects of the order, and where the Commissioners exercise any jurisdiction to make such an order on an application or reference to them, they

may insert any such provisions in the order notwithstanding that the application or reference does not propose their insertion.

(2) Where the Commissioners make an order under this Act, then (without prejudice to the requirements of this Act where the order is subject to appeal) they may themselves give such public notice as they think fit of the making or contents of the order, or may require it to be given by any person on whose application the order is made or by any charity affected by the order.

(3) The Commissioners at any time within twelve months after they have made an order under any provision of this Act other than section 61 if they are satisfied that the order was made by mistake or on misrepresentation or otherwise than in conformity with this Act, may with or without any application or reference to them discharge the order in whole or in part, and subject or not to any savings or other transitional provisions.

(4) Except for the purposes of subsection (3) above or of an appeal under this Act, an order made by the Commissioners under this Act shall be deemed to have been duly and formally made and not be called in question on the ground only of irregularity or informality, but (subject to any further order) have effect according to its tenor.

S.89 – *Extends the Commission's powers to add conditions to orders and schemes even if the trustees' application for the order or scheme did not propose such conditions.*

The Commission may give public notice of any order which it makes. [S.89(2)]

Although an application for an order cannot be withdrawn the Commission can discharge it within 12 months if the order has been made by mistake or as a result of misrepresentation – this does not however apply in relation to dissolution of corporate body under S.61. [S.89(3)]

90 Directions of the Commissioners

(1) Any direction given by the Commissioners under any provision contained in this Act—

    (a) may be varied or revoked by a further direction given under that provision; and

    (b) shall be given in writing.

(2) Sections 88 and 89(1), (2) and (4) above shall apply to any such directions as they apply to an order of the Commissioners.

(3) In subsection (1) above the reference to the Commissioners includes, in relation to a direction under subsection (3) of section 8 above, a reference to any person conducting an inquiry under that section.

(4) Nothing in this section shall be read as applying to any directions contained in an order made by the Commissioners under section 87(1) above.

S.90 – *Allows the Commission to vary directions it has made but not one which requires a default to be made good under S.87(1).*

91 Service of orders and directions

(1) This section applies to any order or direction made or given by the Commissioners under this Act.

(2) An order or direction to which this section applies may be served on a person (other than a body corporate)—

(a) by delivering it to that person;
(b) by leaving it at his last known address in the United Kingdom; or
(c) by sending it by post to him at that address.

(3) An order or direction to which this section applies may be served on a body corporate by delivering it or sending it by post—

(a) to the registered or principal office of the body in the United Kingdom, or
(b) if it has no such office in the United Kingdom, to any place in the United Kingdom where it caries on business or conducts its activities (as the case may be).

(4) Any such order or direction may also be served on a person (including a body corporate) by sending it by post to that person at an address notified by that person to the Commissioners for the purposes of this subsection.

(5) In this section any reference to the Commissioners includes, in relation to a direction given under subsection (3) of section 8 above, a reference to any person conducting an inquiry under that section.

S.91 – *Provides that directions and orders can be served by the Commission at a person's last known address in the UK or his last notified address.*

92 Appeals from Commissioners

(1) Provision shall be made by rules of court for regulating appeals to the High Court under this Act against orders or decisions of the Commissioners.

(2) On such an appeal the Attorney General shall be entitled to appear and be heard, and such other persons as the rules allow or as the court may direct.

> **S.92** – *Appeals against orders or decisions of the Commission are to the High Court and the Attorney General is entitled to appear. Indeed, under Civil Procedure Rules he has to do so and should be approached through the Treasury Solicitor who acts for the Attorney General. Other persons interested can also be heard by the Court, for example, someone removed by an order of the Commission – see S.16(12).*

93 Miscellaneous provisions as to evidence

(1) Where, in any proceedings to recover or compel payment of any rentcharge or other periodical payment claimed by or on behalf of a charity out of land or of the rents, profits or other income of land, otherwise than as rent incident to a reversion, it is shown that the rentcharge or other periodical payment has at any time been paid for twelve consecutive years to or for the benefit of the charity, that shall be prima facie evidence of the perpetual liability to it of the land or income, and no proof of its origin shall be necessary.

(2) In any proceedings, the following documents, that is to say,—

    (a) the printed copies of the reports of the Commissioners for enquiring concerning charities, 1818 to 1837, who were appointed under the Act 58 Geo 3 c 91 and subsequent Acts; and

    (b) the printed copies of the reports which were made for various counties and county boroughs to the Charity Commissioners by their assistant commissioners and presented to the House of Commons as returns to orders of various dates beginning with 8th December 1890, and ending with 9th September 1909,

shall be admissible as evidence of the documents and facts stated in them.

(3) Evidence of any order, certificate or other document issued by the Commissioners may be given by means of a copy retained by them, or taken from a copy so retained, and certified to be a true copy by any officer of the Commissioners generally or specially authorised by them to act for this purpose; and a document purporting to be such a copy shall be received in evidence without proof of the official position, authority or handwriting of the person certifying it.

S.93 – *Contains miscellaneous provisions as to evidence and, for example, allows a Court to accept certified copies of reports, orders, certificates and other documents issued by the Commission over the years without an officer of the Commission having to attend Court in person.*

94 Restriction on institution of proceedings for certain offences

(1) No proceedings for an offence under this Act to which this section applies shall be instituted except by or with the consent of the Director of Public Prosecutions.

(2) This section applies to any offence under—

    (a) section 5;
    (b) section 11;
    (c) section 18(14);
    (d) section 49; or
    (e) section 73(1).

S.94 – *To ensure that criminal prosecutions are commenced only in serious cases, the consent of the Director of Public Prosecutions is required before a criminal prosecution is undertaken in relation to:-*

- *S.5 (statement of registered status)*

- *S.11 (provision of false or misleading information to the Commisson)*

- *S.14 (failure to obey a stop or freezing order)*

- *S.49 (failure to submit an annual report or return or to supply the public with accounts)*

- *S.73(1) (acting as a trustee while disqualified)*

95 Offences by bodies corporate

Where any offence under this Act is committed by a body corporate and is proved to have been committed with the consent or connivance of, or to be attributable to any neglect on the part of, any director, manager, secretary or other similar officer of the body corporate, or any person who was purporting to act in any such capacity, he as well as the body corporate shall be guilty of that offence and shall be liable to be proceeded against and punished accordingly.

In relation to a body corporate whose affairs are managed by its members, "director" means a member of the body corporate.

S.95 – *Where a company has committed an offence under the Act, an appropriate officer, usually a director, can also be prosecuted.*

96 Construction of references to a "charity" or to particular classes of charity

(1) In this Act, except in so far as the context otherwise requires—

"charity" means any institution, corporate or not, which is established for charitable purposes and is subject to the control of the High Court in the exercise of the court's jurisdiction with respect to charities;

"ecclesiastical charity" has the same meaning as in the Local Government Act 1894;

"exempt charity" means (subject to section 24(8) above) a charity comprised in Schedule 2 to this Act;

"local charity" means, in relation to any area, a charity established for purposes which are by their nature or by the trusts of the charity directed wholly or mainly to the benefit of that area or of part of it;

"parochial charity" means, in relation to any parish or (in Wales) community, a charity the benefits of which are, or the separate distribution of the benefits of which is, confined to inhabitants of the parish or community, or of a single ancient ecclesiastical parish which included that parish or community or part of it, or of an area consisting of that parish or community with not more than four neighbouring parishes or communities.

(2) The expression "charity" is not in this Act applicable—

(a) to any ecclesiastical corporation (that is to say, any corporation in the Church of England, whether sole or aggregate, which is established for spiritual purposes) in respect of the corporate property of the corporation, except to a corporation aggregate having some purposes which are not ecclesiastical in respect of its corporate property held for those purposes; or

(b) to any Diocesan Board of Finance within the meaning of the Endowments and Glebe Measure 1976 for any diocese in respect of the diocesan glebe land of that diocese within the meaning of that Measure; or

(c) to any trust of property for purposes for which the property has been consecrated.

(3) A charity shall be deemed for the purposes of this Act to have a permanent endowment unless all property held for the purposes of the charity may be expended for those purposes without distinction between capital and income, and in this Act "permanent endowment" means, in relation to any charity, property held subject to a restriction on its being expended for the purposes of the charity.

(4) References in this Act to a charity whose income from all sources does not in aggregate amount to more than a specified amount shall be construed—

    (a) by reference to the gross revenues of the charity, or

    (b) if the Commissioners so determine, by reference to the amount which they estimate to be the likely amount of those revenues,

but without (in either case) bringing into account anything for the yearly value of land occupied by the charity apart from the pecuniary income (if any) received from that land; and any question as to the application of any such reference to a charity shall be determined by the Commissioners, whose decision shall be final.

(5) The Commissioners may direct that for all or any of the purposes of this Act an institution established for any special purposes of or in connection with a charity (being charitable purposes) shall be treated as forming part of that charity or as forming a distinct charity.

[(6) The Commissioners may direct that for all or any of the purposes of this Act two or more charities having the same charity trustees shall be treated as a single charity.]

S.96 – *S.96(1) interprets various references to charities or types of charity, for example:-*

- *a statutory definition of "charity" by reference to case law;*

- *income from all sources means gross revenues*

- *a charity does not include any corporation in the Church of England*

S.96(3) gives statutory definition to "permanent endowment", unhelpfully in the negative, so that a charity is deemed to have permanent endowment unless all its property may be spent irrespective of whether it is income or capital. The whole question of permanent endowment, particularly in relation to investment policy is now being considered within the charity sector.

Under S.96(5) the Commission can decide that a special trust held by a charity is either a subsidiary or a distinct charity. In practice charities linked in this way must be identified with the same charitable activity.

Under S.96(6) the Commission may, in what is known as a "uniting direction", direct that two or more charities which have the same trustees may be grouped together for some or all of the purposes of the Acts. This would result in an administrative grouping rather than a legal merger of the charities involved. Although the basis for such a uniting direction is common trusteeship, in practice the charities so united must have broadly similar purposes.

97 General interpretation

(1) In this Act, except in so far as the context otherwise requires—

"charitable purposes" means purposes which are exclusively charitable according to the law of England and Wales;

"charity trustees" means the persons having the general control and management of the administration of a charity;

"the Commissioners" means the Charity Commissioners for England and Wales;

"company" means a company formed and registered under the Companies Act 1985 or to which the provisions of that Act apply as they apply to such a company;

"the court" means the High Court and, within the limits of its jurisdiction, any other court in England and Wales having a jurisdiction in respect of charities concurrent (within any limit of area or amount) with that of the High Court, and includes any judge or officer of the court exercising the jurisdiction of the court;

"financial year"—

(a) in relation to a charity which is a company, shall be construed in accordance with section 223 of the Companies Act 1985; and

(b) in relation to any other charity, shall be construed in accordance with regulations made by virtue of section 42(2) above;

but this definition is subject to the transitional provisions in section 99(4) below and Part II of Schedule 8 to this Act;

"gross income", in relation to charity, means its gross recorded income from all sources including special trusts;

"independent examiner", in relation to a charity, means such a person as is mentioned in section 43(3)(a) above;

"institution" includes any trust or undertaking;

"the official custodian" means the official custodian for charities;

"permanent endowment" shall be construed in accordance with section 96(3) above;

"the register" means the register of charities kept under section 3 above and "registered" shall be construed accordingly;

"special trust" means property which is held and administered by or on behalf of a charity for any special purposes of the charity, and is so held and administered on separate trusts relating only to that property but a special trust shall not, by itself, constitute a charity for the purposes of Part VI of this Act;

"trusts" in relation to a charity, means the provisions establishing it as a charity and regulating its purposes and administration, whether those provisions take effect by way of trust or not, and in relation to other institutions has a corresponding meaning.

(2) In this Act, except in so far as the context otherwise requires, "document" includes information recorded in any form, and, in relation to information recorded otherwise than in legible form—

   (a) any reference to its production shall be construed as a reference to the furnishing of a copy of it in legible form; and

   (b) any reference to the furnishing of a copy of, or extract from, it shall accordingly be construed as a reference to the furnishing of a copy of, or extract from, it in legible form.

(3) No vesting or transfer of any property in pursuance of any provision of Part IV or IX of this Act shall operate as a breach of a covenant or condition against alienation or give rise to a forfeiture.

S.97 – *This section contains several interpretations, some more useful than others, for example:-*

- *"charitable purposes" means purposes which are exclusively charitable under the law of England and Wales, a somewhat circular definition referred to in the Introduction;*

- *"charity trustees" mean the persons having the general control and management of the administration of a charity. As mentioned in the Introduction it does not matter what a trustee is called; if he is in control, he is a trustee.*

- *"special trust" means property which is set aside for any special purposes of a charity but which is not of itself a separate charity.*

98 Consequential amendments and repeals

(1) The enactments mentioned in Schedule 6 to this Act shall be amended as provided in that Schedule.

(2) The enactments mentioned in Schedule 7 to this Act are hereby repealed to the extent specified in the third column of the Schedule.

S.98 – *Deals with consequential amendments to and repeals of other legislation.*

99 Commencement and transitional provisions

(1) Subject to subsection (2) below this Act shall come into force on 1st August 1993.

(2) Part VI, section 69 and paragraph 21(3) of Schedule 6 shall not come into force until such day as the Secretary of State may by order appoint; and different days may be appointed for different provisions or different purposes.

(3) Until the coming into force of all the provisions mentioned in subsection (2) above the provisions mentioned in Part I of Schedule 8 to this Act shall continue in force notwithstanding their repeal.

(4) Part II of Schedule 8 to this Act shall have effect until the coming into force of the first regulations made by virtue of section 42(2) above for determining the financial year of a charity for the purposes of the provisions mentioned in that Part.

S.99 – *Deals with the commencement of the Act, all of which is now in force (see the Charities Act 1993 (Commencement and Transitional Provisions Order 1995 (S.I.2695)*

100 Short title and extent

(1) This Act may be cited as the Charities Act 1993.

(2) Subject to subsection (3) to (6) below, this Act extends only to England and Wales.

(3) Section 10 above and this section extend to the whole of the United Kingdom.

(4) Section 15(2) extends also to Northern Ireland.

(5) Sections 70 and 71 and so much of section 86 as relates to those sections extend also to Scotland.

(6) The amendments in Schedule 6 and the repeals in Schedule 7 have the same extent as the enactments to which they refer and section 98 above extends accordingly.

S.100 – *Confirms that, apart from specific instances, the Act applies only to England and Wales*

Schedule 1

Constitution etc of Charity Commissioners

Section 1

1

(1) There shall be a Chief Charity Commissioner and two other commissioners.

(2) Two at least of the commissioners shall be persons who have a seven year general qualification within the meaning of section 71 of the Courts and Legal Services Act 1990.

(3) The chief commissioner and the other commissioners shall be appointed by the Secretary of State, and shall be deemed for all purposes to be employed in the civil service of the Crown.

(4) There may be paid to each of the commissioners such salary and allowances as the Secretary of State may with the approval of the Treasury determine.

(5) If at any time it appears to the Secretary of State that there should be more than three commissioners, he may with the approval of the Treasury appoint not more than two additional commissioners.

2

(1) The chief commissioner may, with the approval of the Treasury as to number and conditions of service, appoint such assistant commissioners and other officers and such employees as he thinks necessary for the proper discharge of the functions of the Commissioners and of the official custodian.

(2) There may be paid to officers and employees so appointed such salaries or remuneration as the Treasury may determine.

3

(1) The Commissioners may use an official seal for the authentication of documents, and their seal shall be officially and judicially noticed.

(2) The Documentary Evidence Act 1868, as amended by the Documentary Evidence Act 1882, shall have effect as if in the Schedule to the Act of 1868 the Commissioners were included in the first column and any commissioner or assistant commissioner and any officer authorised to act on behalf of the Commissioners were mentioned in the second column.

(3) The Commissioners shall have power to regulate their own procedure and, subject to any such regulations and to any directions of the chief commissioner, any one commissioner or any assistant commissioner may act for and in the name of the Commissioners.

(4) Where the Commissioners act as a board, then—

    (a) if not more than four commissioners hold office for the time being, the quorum shall be two commissioners (of whom at least one must be a person having a qualification such as is mentioned in paragraph 1(2) above); and

    (b) if five commissioners so hold office, the quorum shall be three commissioners (of whom at least one must be a person having such a qualification);

and in the case of an equality of votes the chief commissioner or in his absence the commissioner presiding shall have a second or casting vote.

(5) The Commissioners shall have power to act notwithstanding any vacancy in their number.

(6) It is hereby declared that the power of a commissioner or assistant commissioner to act for and in the name of the Commissioners in accordance with sub-paragraph (3) above may, in particular, be exercised in relation to functions of the Commissioners under sections 8, 18, 19 and 63 of this Act, including functions under sections 8, 18 and 19 as applied by section 80(1).

4

Legal proceedings may be instituted by or against the Commissioners by the name of the Charity Commissioners for England and Wales, and shall not abate or be affected by any change in the persons who are the commissioners.

Schedule 1
Sets out the constitution of the Commission which in effect is the Chief Charity Commissioner and four other Commissioners of whom two must be lawyers. At present there are three full-time Commissioners and two part-time Commissioners. The Commission's sponsoring department is the Home Office but numbers and salaries of employees are subject to Treasury control.

Legal proceedings by or against the Commission should be taken in the name of the Charity Commissioners for England and Wales. The Commission can appoint Assistant Commissioners to exercise certain powers under the Act. The Board of Commissioners generally delegate powers by Division (i.e. Support, Investigation, Registration) and then, by grade, to staff within that Division. The scope of powers exercisable by given Assistant Commissioners will be limited until the officer concerned has demonstrated competence to handle particular functions.

SCHEDULE 2

EXEMPT CHARITIES

Sections 3, 96

The following institutions, so far as they are charities, are exempt charities within the meaning of this Act, that is to say—

(a) any institution which, if the Charities Act 1960 had not been passed, would be exempted from the powers and jurisdiction, under the Charitable Trusts Acts 1853 to 1939, of the Commissioners or Minister of Education (apart from any power of the Commissioners or Minister to apply those Acts in whole or in part to charities otherwise exempt) by the terms of any enactment not contained in those Acts other than section 9 of the Places of Worship Registration Act 1855;

(b) the universities of Oxford, Cambridge, London, Durham and Newcastle, the colleges and halls in the universities of Oxford, Cambridge, Durham and Newcastle, Queen Mary and Westfield College in the University of London and the colleges of Winchester and Eton;

(c) any university, university college, or institution connected with a university or university college, which Her Majesty declares by Order in Council to be an exempt charity for the purposes of this Act;

(d) . . .

[(da)   the Qualifications and Curriculum Authority;]

(e) . . .;

[(f) the Qualifications, Curriculum and Assessment Authority for Wales;]

(g) . . .;

(h) . . .;

(i) a successor company to a higher education corporation (within the meaning of section 129(5) of the Education Reform Act 1988) at a time when an institution conducted by the company is for the time being designated under that section;

(j) . . .;

(k) the Board of Trustees of the Victoria and Albert Museum;

(l) the Board of Trustees of the Science Museum;

(m) the Board of Trustees of the Armouries;

(n) the Board of Trustees of the Royal Botanic Gardens, Kew;

(o) the Board of Trustees of the National Museums and Galleries on Merseyside;

(p) the trustees of the British Museum and the trustees of the Natural History Museum;

(q) the Board of Trustees of the National Gallery;

(r) the Board of Trustees of the Tate Gallery;

(s) the Board of Trustees of the National Portrait Gallery;

(t) the Board of Trustees of the Wallace Collection;

(u) the Trustees of the Imperial War Museum;

(v) the Trustees of the National Maritime Museum;

(w) any institution which is administered by or on behalf of an institution included above and is established for the general purposes of, or for any special purpose of or in connection with, the last-mentioned institution;

(x) the Church Commissioners and any institution which is administered by them;

(y) any registered society within the meaning of the Industrial and Provident Societies Act 1965 and any registered society or branch within the meaning of the Friendly Societies Act 1974;

(z) the Board of Governors of the Museum of London;

(za) the British Library Board;

[(zb) the National Lottery Charities Board.]

Schedule 2

Lists exempt charities to include:-

* *further and higher education corporations;*

* *universities who have undertaken to submit accounts to the Higher Education Funding Councils;*

* *the Church Commissioners;*

* *Industrial and Provident Societies and*

* *certain national museums and other bodies.*

Foundation and voluntary aided schools are also exempt by virtue of the Schools Standards and Framework Act 1998

SCHEDULE 3

ENLARGEMENT OF AREAS OF LOCAL CHARITIES

Section 13

Existing area	Permissible enlargement
1. Greater London	Any area comprising Greater London.
2. Any area in Greater London and not in, or partly in, the City of London.	(i) Any area in Greater London and not in, or partly in, the City of London;
	(ii) the area of Greater London exclusive of the City of London;
	(iii) any area comprising the area of Greater London, exclusive of the City of London;

Existing area	Permissible enlargement
	(iv) any area partly in Greater London and partly in any adjacent parish or parishes (civil or ecclesiastical), and not partly in the City of London.
3. A district	Any area comprising the district
[3A. A Welsh county or county borough	Any area comprising that county or county borough.]
4. Any area in a district	(i) Any area in the district;
	(ii) the district;
	(iii) any area comprising the district;
	(iv) any area partly in the district and partly in any adjacent district [or in any adjacent Welsh county or county borough].
[4A. Any area in a Welsh county or county borough	(i) Any area in the county or county borough;
	(ii) the county or county borough;
	(iii) any area comprising the county or county borough;
	(iv) any area partly in the county or county borough and partly in any adjacent Welsh county or county borough or in any adjacent district.]
5. A parish (civil or ecclesiastical), or two or more parishes, or an area in a parish, or partly in each of two or more parishes.	Any area not extending beyond the parish or parishes comprising or adjacent to the area in column 1.
6. In Wales, a community, or two or more communities, or an area in a community, or partly in each of two or more communities.	Any area not extending beyond the community or communities comprising or adjacent to the area in column 1.

Schedule 3
Lists contain local authority areas for the purpose of S.13(4)

SCHEDULE 4

COURT'S JURISDICTION OVER CERTAIN CHARITIES GOVERNED BY OR UNDER STATUTE

Section 15

1

The court may by virtue of section 15(3) of this Act exercise its jurisdiction with respect to charities—

    (a) in relation to charities established or regulated by any provision of the Seamen's Fund Winding-up Act 1851 which is repealed by the Charities Act 1960;

    (b) in relation to charities established or regulated by schemes under the Endowed Schools Act 1869 to 1948, or section 75 of the Elementary Education Act 1870 or by schemes given effect under section 2 of the Education Act 1973 [or section 554 of the Education Act 1996];

    (c) . . .

    (d) in relation to fuel allotments, that is to say, land which, by any enactment relating to inclosure or any instrument having effect under such an enactment, is vested in trustees upon trust that the land or the rents and profits of the land shall be used for the purpose of providing poor persons with fuel;

    (e) in relation to charities established or regulated by any provision of the Municipal Corporations Act 1883 which is repealed by the Charities Act 1960 or by any scheme having effect under any such provision;

    (f) in relation to charities regulated by schemes under the London Government Act 1899;

    (g) in relation to charities established or regulated by orders or regulations under section 2 of the Regimental Charitable Funds Act 1935;

    (h) in relation to charities regulated by section 79 of this Act, or by any such order as is mentioned in that section.

2

Notwithstanding anything in section 19 of the Commons Act 1876 a scheme for the administration of a fuel allotment (within the meaning of the foregoing paragraph) may provide—

    (a) for the sale or letting of the allotment or any part thereof, for the discharge of the land sold or let from any restrictions as to the use thereof imposed by or under any enactment relating to inclosure and for the application of the sums payable to the trustees of the allotment in respect of the sale or lease; or

    (b) for the exchange of the allotment or any part thereof for other land, for the discharge as aforesaid of the land given in exchange by the said trustees, and for the application of any money payable to the said trustees for equality of exchange; or

(c) for the use of the allotment or any part thereof for any purposes specified in the scheme.

Schedule 4
Lists charities created by statute and not requiring the complicated S.17 procedure for amendment by the Commission. In the main this relates to allotment and regimental charities and charities governed by schemes under the Endowed Schools Act.

SCHEDULE 5

MEANING OF "CONNECTED PERSON" FOR PURPOSES OF SECTION 36(2)

Section 36(2)

1

In section 36(2) of this Act "connected person", in relation to a charity, means—

(a) a charity trustee or trustee for the charity;

(b) a person who is the donor of any land to the charity (whether the gift was made on or after the establishment of the charity);

(c) a child, parent, grandchild, grandparent, brother or sister of any such trustee or donor;

(d) an officer, agent or employee of the charity;

(e) the spouse of any person falling within any of sub-paragraphs (a) to (d) above;

(f) an institution which is controlled—
 (i) by any person failing within any of sub-paragraphs (a) to (e) above, or
 (ii) by two or more such persons taken together; or

(g) a body corporate in which—
 (i) any connected person falling within any of sub-paragraphs (a) to (f) above has a substantial interest, or
 (ii) two or more such persons, taken together, have a substantial interest.

2

(1) In paragraph 1(c) above "child" includes a stepchild and an illegitimate child.

(2) For the purposes of paragraph 1(e) above a person living with another as that person's husband or wife shall be treated as that person's spouse.

3

For the purposes of paragraph 1(f) above a person controls an institution if he is able to secure that the affairs of the institution are conducted in accordance with his wishes.

4

(1) For the purposes of paragraph 1(g) above any such connected person as is there mentioned has a substantial interest in a body corporate if the person or institution in question—

    (a) is interested in shares comprised in the equity share capital of that body of a nominal value of more than one-fifth of that share capital, or

    (b) is entitled to exercise, or control the exercise of, more than one-fifth of the voting power at any general meeting of that body.

(2) The rules set out in Part I of Schedule 13 to the Companies Act 1985 (rules for interpretation of certain provisions of that Act) shall apply for the purposes of sub-paragraph (1) above as they apply for the purposes of section 346(4) of that Act ("connected persons" etc).

(3) In this paragraph "equity share capital" and "share" have the same meaning as in that Act.

> **Schedule 5**
> *Defines "a connected person" for the purpose of S.36 (disposals of land). The definition effectively includes a charity's trading subsidiary, so a disposal of land to such a subsidiary will need commission consent.*

SCHEDULE 6

CONSEQUENTIAL AMENDMENTS

Section 98(1)

Repealed in part, in relation to England and Wales, by the Housing Act 1996, s 227, Sch 19, Part I.

Repealed in part, in relation to England and Wales, by SI 1996/2325, ar4(1), Sch 1, Part I.

Repealed in part by the Finance Act 1999, s 139, Sch 20, Pt V(5).

Date in force: this repeal has effect in relation to instruments executed on or after 6 February 2000: see the Finance Act 1999, Sch 20, Pt V(5).

SCHEDULE 7

REPEALS

Section 98(2)

Chapter	Short title	Extent of repeal
35 & 36 Vic. c.24.	The Charitable Trustees Incorporation Act 1872.	The whole Act so far as unrepealed.
10 & 11 Geo.5. c.16.	The Imperial War Museum Act 1920.	Section 5.
24 &25 Geo.5. c.43.	The National Maritime Museum Act 1934.	Section 7.

8 & 9 Eliz.2 c.58.	The Charities Act 1960	The whole Act so far as unrepealed except-
		  section 28(9)
		  section 35(6)
		  section 38(3) to (5)
		  section 39(2)
		  sections 48 and 49
		  Schedule 6.

1963 c.33.	The London Government Act 1963.	Section 81(9)(b) and (c).
1963 c.xi.	The Universities of Durham and Newcastle-upon-Tyne Act 1963.	Section 10.
1965 c.17.	The Museum of London Act 1965.	Section 11.
1972 c.54.	The British Library Act 1972.	Section 4(2).
1972 c.70.	The Local Government Act 1972.	Section 210(9).
1973 c.16.	The Education Act 1973.	In section 2(7) the words from "but" onwards. In Schedule 1, paragraph 1(1) and (3).
1976 No.4.	The Endowments and Glebe Measure 1976.	Section 44.
1983 c.47.	The National Heritage Act 1983.	In Schedule 5, paragraph 4.

Chapter	Short title	Extent of repeal
1985 c.9.	The Companies Consolidation (Consequential Provisions) Act 1985.	In Schedule 2 the entry relating to the Charities Act 1960.
1985 c.20.	The Charities Act 1985.	Section 1.
1986 c.60. ·	The Financial Services Act 1986.	In Schedule 16, paragraph 1.
1988 c.40.	The Education Reform Act 1988.	In Schedule 12, paragraphs 9, 10, 63 and 64.
1989 c.40.	The Companies Act 1989.	Section 111.
1989 c.xiii.	The Queen Mary and Westfield College Act 1989.	Section 10.
1990 c.41.	The Courts and Legal Services Act 1990.	In Schedule 10, paragraph 14.
1992 c. 13.	The Further and Higher Education Act 1992.	In Schedule 8, paragraph 69.
1992 c.41.	The Charities Act 1992.	The whole of Part I except- section 1(1) and (4) sections 29 and 30 section 36 sections 49 and 50 Section 75(b). Section 76(1)(a). In section 77, subsections (2)(a), (b) and (c) and in subsection (4) the figures 20, 22 and 23. Section 79(4) and (5). Schedules 1 to 4. In Schedule 6, paragraph 13(2). In Schedule 7, the entries relating to section 8 of the Charities Act 1960 and (so far as not in force at the date specified in section 99(1) of this Act) the Charities Act 1985.

Chapter	Short title	Extent of repeal
1992 c.44.	The Museums and Galleries Act 1992.	In Schedule 8, paragraphs 4 and 10.
		In Schedule 9, the entry relating to the Charities Act 1960.

SCHEDULE 8

TRANSITIONAL PROVISIONS

Section 99(3), (4)

PART I

PROVISIONS APPLYING PENDING COMING INTO FORCE OF PART VI ETC

1 In the Charities Act 1960—

section 8
section 32
Part V so far as relevant to those sections.

2 In the Charities Act 1985

section 1
sections 6 and 7 so far as relevant to section 1.

PART II

PROVISIONS APPLYING PENDING COMING INTO FORCE OF "FINANCIAL YEAR" REGULATIONS

Section 5

In section 5(1) of this Act "financial year"—

(a) in relation to a charity which is a company, shall be construed in accordance with section 223 of the Companies Act 1985;
(b) in relation to any other charity, means any period in respect of which an income and expenditure account is required to be prepared whether under section 32 of the Charities Act 1960 or by or under the authority of any other Act, whether that period is a year or not.

Sections 74 and 75

In sections 74(1)(a) and 75(1)(b) of this Act "financial year" means any period in respect of which an income and expenditure account is required to be prepared whether under section 32 of the Charities Act 1960 or by or under the authority of any other Act, whether that period is a year or not.

Schedules 6, 7 and 8 are no longer of any practical interest.

Charities Act 1992

An Act to amend the Charities Act 1960 and make other provision with respect to charities; to regulate fund-raising activities carried on in connection with charities and other institutions; to make fresh provision with respect to public charitable collections; and for connected purposes

[16th March 1992]

BE IT ENACTED by the Queen's most Excellent Majesty, by and with the advice and consent of the Lords Spiritual and Temporal, and Commons, in this present Parliament assembled, and by the authority of the same, as follows:–

PART I

CHARITIES

In theory the following sections in Part I remain in force but they are not considered relevant for the purposes of this Commentary:-

Sections 29 and 30 – the investment role of the Official Custodian

Sections 36 and 50 – removal of certain requirements for Charity Commission consent, whether in trusts or statutes.

Charity property

29 Divestment of charity property held by official custodian for charities

(1) The official custodian shall, in accordance with this section, divest himself of all property to which this subsection applies.

(2) Subsection (1) applies to any property held by the official custodian in his capacity as such, with the exception of—

(a) any land; and

(b) any property (other than land) which is vested in him by virtue of an order of the Commissioners under section 20 of the 1960 Act [or section 18 of the Charities Act 1993] (power to act for protection of charities).

(3) Where property to which subsection (1) applies is held by the official custodian in trust for particular charities, he shall (subject to subsection (7)) divest himself of that property in such manner as the Commissioners may direct.

(4) Without prejudice to the generality of subsection (3), directions given by the Commissioners under that subsection may make different provision in relation to different property held by the official custodian or in relation to different classes or descriptions of property held by him, including (in particular)—

(a) provision designed to secure that the divestment required by subsection (1) is effected in stages or by means of transfers or other disposals taking place at different times;

(b) provision requiring the official custodian to transfer any specified investments, or any specified class or description of investments, held by him in trust for a charity—

(i) to the charity trustees or any trustee for the charity, or

(ii) to a person nominated by the charity trustees to hold any such investments in trust for the charity;

(c) provision requiring the official custodian to sell or call in any specified investments, or any specified class or description of investments, so held by him and to pay any proceeds of sale or other money accruing therefrom—

(i) to the charity trustees or any trustee for the charity, or

(ii) into any bank account kept in its name.

(5) The charity trustees of a charity may, in the case of any property falling to be transferred by the official custodian in accordance with a direction under subsection (3), nominate a person to hold any such property in trust for the charity; but a person shall not be so nominated unless—

(a) if an individual, he resides in England and Wales; or

(b) if a body corporate, it has a place of business there.

(6) Directions under subsection (3) shall, in the case of any property vested in the official custodian by virtue of section 22(6) of the 1960 Act (common investment funds), provide for any such property to be transferred—

(a) to the trustees appointed to manage the common investment fund concerned; or

(b) to any person nominated by those trustees who is authorised by or under the common investment scheme concerned to hold that fund or any part of it.

(7) Where the official custodian—

(a) holds any relevant property in trust for a charity, but

    (b) after making reasonable inquiries is unable to locate the charity or any of its trustees,

he shall—

    (i) unless the relevant property is money, sell the property and hold the proceeds of sale pending the giving by the Commissioners of a direction under subsection (8);

    (ii) if the relevant property is money, hold it pending the giving of any such direction;

and for this purpose "relevant property" means any property to which subsection (1) applies or any proceeds of sale or other money accruing to the official custodian in consequence of a direction under subsection (3).

(8) Where subsection (7) applies in relation to a charity ("the dormant charity"), the Commissioners may direct the official custodian—

    (a) to pay such amount as is held by him in accordance with that subsection to such other charity as is specified in the direction in accordance with subsection (9), or

    (b) to pay to each of two or more other charities so specified in the direction such part of that amount as is there specified in relation to that charity.

(9) The Commissioners may specify in a direction under subsection (8) such charity or charities as they consider appropriate, being in each case a charity whose purposes are, in the opinion of the Commissioners, as similar in character to those of the dormant charity as is reasonably practicable; but the Commissioners shall not so specify any charity unless they have received from the charity trustees written confirmation that they are willing to accept the amount proposed to be paid to the charity.

(10) Any amount received by a charity by virtue of subsection (8) shall be received by the charity on terms that—

    (a) it shall be held and applied by the charity for the purposes of the charity, but

    (b) it shall, as property of the charity, nevertheless be subject to any restrictions on expenditure to which it, or (as the case may be) the property which it represents, was subject as property of the dormant charity.

(11) At such time as the Commissioners are satisfied that the official custodian has divested himself of all property held by him in trust for particular charities, all remaining funds held by him as official custodian shall be paid by him into the Consolidated Fund.

(12) Nothing in subsection (11) applies in relation to any property held by the official custodian which falls within subsection (2)(a) or (b).

(13) In this section "land" does not include any interest in land by way of mortgage or other security.

30 Provisions supplementary to s 29

(1) Any directions of the Commissioners under section 29 above shall have effect notwithstanding anything—

    (a) in the trusts of a charity, or

    (b) in section 17(1) of the 1960 Act [or section 22(1) of the Charities Act 1993] (supplementary provisions as to property vested in official custodian).

(2) Subject to subsection (3), any provision—

    (a) of the trusts of a charity, or

    (b) of any directions given by an order of the Commissioners made in connection with a transaction requiring the sanction of an order under section 29(1) of the 1960 Act (restrictions on dealing with charity property),

shall cease to have effect if and to the extent that it requires or authorises personal property of the charity to be transferred to or held by the official custodian; and for this purpose "personal property" extends to any mortgage or other real security, but does not include any interest in land other than such an interest by way of mortgage or other security.

(3) Subsection (2) does not apply to—

    (a) any provision of an order made under section 20 of the 1960 Act [or section 18 of the Charities Act 1993] (power to act for protection of charities); or

    (b) any provision of any other order, or of any scheme, of the Commissioners if the provision requires trustees of a charity to make payments into an account maintained by the official custodian with a view to the accumulation of a sum as capital of the charity (whether or not by way of recoupment of a sum expended out of the charity's permanent endowment);

but any such provision as is mentioned in paragraph (b) shall have effect as if, instead of requiring the trustees to make such payments into an account maintained by the official custodian, it required the trustees to make such payments into an account maintained by them or by any other person (apart from the official custodian) who is either a trustee for the charity or a person nominated by them to hold such payments in trust for the charity.

(4) The disposal of any property by the official custodian in accordance with section 29 above shall operate to discharge him from his trusteeship of that property.

(5) Where any instrument issued by the official custodian in connection with any such disposal contains a printed reproduction of his official seal, that instrument shall have the same effect as if it were duly sealed with his official seal.

36 Removal of requirements under statutory provisions for consent to dealings with charity land

(1) Any provision—

(a) establishing or regulating a particular charity and contained in, or having effect under, any Act of Parliament, or

(b) contained in the trusts of a charity,

shall cease to have effect if and to the extent that it provides for dispositions of, or other dealings with, land held by or in trust for the charity to require the consent of the Commissioners (whether signified by order or otherwise).

(2) Any provision of an order or scheme under the Education Act 1944 or the Education Act 1973 relating to a charity shall cease to have effect if and to the extent that it requires, in relation to any sale, lease or other disposition of land held by or in trust for the charity, approval by the Commissioners or the Secretary of State of the amount for which the land is to be sold, leased or otherwise disposed of.

(3) In this section "land" means land in England or Wales.

50 Contributions towards maintenance etc of almshouses

(1) Any provision in the trusts of an almshouse charity which relates to the payment by persons resident in the charity's almshouses of contributions towards the cost of maintaining those almshouses and essential services in them shall cease to have effect if and to the extent that it provides for the amount, or the maximum amount, of such contributions to be a sum specified, approved or authorised by the Commissioners.

(2) In subsection (1)—

"almshouse" means any premises maintained as an almshouse, whether they are called an almshouse or not; and

"almshouse charity" means a charity which is authorised under its trusts to maintain almshouses.

PART II

CONTROL OF FUND-RAISING FOR CHARITABLE INSTITUTIONS

Part II: Control of Fund Raising for Charitable Institutions.
Control of fund raising is to be achieved by having prescribed agreements with "commercial participators" or "professional fund-raisers," (as defined below) which ensure:-

- *disclosure of information to the public*

- *refunds to donors in certain circumstances*

- *prohibition of unacceptable fund-raising methods*

> *A prescribed agreement has to contain certain provisions but is not in a standard or model form*

Preliminary

58 Interpretation of Part II

(1) In this Part—

"charitable contributions", in relation to any representation made by any commercial participator or other person, means—

(a) the whole or part of—
    (i) the consideration given for goods or services sold or supplied by him, or
    (ii) any proceeds (other than such consideration) of a promotional venture undertaken by him, or
(b) sums given by him by way of donation in connection with the sale or supply of any such goods or services (whether the amount of such sums is determined by reference to the value of any such goods or services or otherwise);

"charitable institution" means a charity or an institution (other than a charity) which is established for charitable, benevolent or philanthropic purposes;

"charity" means a charity within the meaning of [the Charities Act 1993];

"commercial participator", in relation to any charitable institution, means any person [(apart from a company connected with the institution)] who—

(a) carries on for gain a business other than a fund-raising business, but
(b) in the course of that business, engages in any promotional venture in the course of which it is represented that charitable contributions are to be given to or applied for the benefit of the institution;

"company" has the meaning given by section [97 of the Charities Act 1993];

"the court" means the High Court or a county court;

"credit card" means a card which is a credit-token within the meaning of the Consumer Credit Act 1974;

"debit card" means a card the use of which by its holder to make a payment results in a current account of his at a bank, or at any other institution providing banking services, being debited with the payment;

"fund-raising business" means any business carried on for gain and wholly or primarily engaged in soliciting or otherwise procuring money or other property for charitable, benevolent or philanthropic purposes;

"institution" includes any trust or undertaking;

"professional fund-raiser" means—

(a) any person (apart from a charitable institution [or a company connected with such an institution]) who carries on a fund-raising business, or

(b) any other person (apart from a person excluded by virtue of subsection (2) or (3)) who for reward solicits money or other property for the benefit of a charitable institution, if he does so otherwise than in the course of any fund-raising venture undertaken by a person falling within paragraph (a) above;

"promotional venture" means any advertising or sales campaign or any other venture undertaken for promotional purposes;

"radio or television programme" includes any item included in a programme service within the meaning of the Broadcasting Act 1990.

(2) In subsection (1), paragraph (b) of the definition of "professional fund-raiser" does not apply to any of the following, namely—

(a) any charitable institution or any company connected with any such institution;

(b) any officer or employee of any such institution or company, or any trustee of any such institution, acting (in each case) in his capacity as such;

(c) any person acting as a collector in respect of a public charitable collection (apart from a person who is to be treated as a promoter of such a collection by virtue of section 65(3));

(d) any person who in the course of a relevant programme, that is to say a radio or television programme in the course of which a fund-raising venture is undertaken by—

(i) a charitable institution, or

(ii) a company connected with such an institution,

makes any solicitation at the instance of that institution or company; or

(e) any commercial participator;

and for this purpose "collector" and "public charitable collection" have the same meaning as in Part III of this Act.

(3) In addition, paragraph (b) of the definition of "professional fund-raiser" does not apply to a person if he does not receive—

(a) more than—

(i) £5 per day, or

(ii) £500 per year,

by way of remuneration in connection with soliciting money or other property for the benefit of the charitable institution referred to in that paragraph; or

(b) more than £500 by way of remuneration in connection with any fund-raising venture in the course of which he solicits money or other property for the benefit of that institution.

(4) In this Part any reference to charitable purposes, where occurring in the context of a reference to charitable, benevolent or philanthropic purposes, is a reference to charitable purposes whether or not the purposes are charitable within the meaning of any rule of law.

(5) For the purposes of this Part a company is connected with a charitable institution if—

(a) the institution, or
(b) the institution and one or more other charitable institutions, taken together,

is or are entitled (whether directly or through one or more nominees) to exercise, or control the exercise of, the whole of the voting power at any general meeting of the company.

(6) In this Part—

(a) "represent" and "solicit" mean respectively represent and solicit in any manner whatever, whether expressly or impliedly and whether done—
   (i) by speaking directly to the person or persons to whom the representation or solicitation is addressed (whether when in his or their presence or not), or
   (ii) by means of a statement published in any newspaper, film or radio or television programme,

   or otherwise, and references to a representation or solicitation shall be construed accordingly; and

(b) any reference to soliciting or otherwise procuring money or other property is a reference to soliciting or otherwise procuring money or other property whether any consideration is, or is to be, given in return for the money or other property or not.

(7) Where—

(a) any solicitation of money or other property for the benefit of a charitable institution is made in accordance with arrangements between any person and that institution, and
(b) under those arrangements that person will be responsible for receiving on behalf of the institution money or other property given in response to the solicitation,

then (if he would not be so regarded apart from this subsection) that person shall be regarded for the purposes of this Part as soliciting money or other property for the benefit of the institution.

(8) Where any fund-raising venture is undertaken by a professional fund-raiser in the course of a radio or television programme, any solicitation which is made by a person in the course of the programme at the instance of the fund-raiser shall be regarded for the purposes of this Part as made by the fund-raiser and not by that person (and shall be so regarded whether or not the solicitation is made by that person for any reward).

(9) In this Part "services" includes facilities, and in particular—

(a) access to any premises or event;
(b) membership of any organisation;
(c) the provision of advertising space; and
(d) the provision of any financial facilities;

and references to the supply of services shall be construed accordingly.

(10) The Secretary of State may by order amend subsection (3) by substituting a different sum for any sum for the time being specified there.

S.58 – *The rules in Part II of the Act affect any "charitable institution" which means not only a charity (registered or not) but also any institution which is established for charitable benevolent or philanthropic purposes.*

*The rules seek to control the activities of any individual or organisation who seeks to derive profit by raising funds for charitable institutions; they do **not** apply to charities who run their own fund-raising activities.*

There are two types of business person which the Act seeks to control:-

(1) "Commercial Participator" ("CP") who is someone who runs a business other than fund-raising and who represents in the course of a promotional venture that contributions will be made to a charitable institution. For example, a bank which operates an affinity card scheme or a manufacturer who offers to make a contribution to charity for every product sold.

(2) "Professional Fund-Raiser" ("PFR") who is someone who for personal gain seeks money or property for a charitable institution, though this definition specifically excludes the charitable institution itself, its trustees, employees, volunteers, trading company and those who receive small honoraria within certain limits (e.g. £5 a day). Also excluded are those who run TV and radio appeals, for example "the Weekly Good Cause" on BBC Radio 4.

Control of fund-raising

59 Prohibition on professional fund-raiser etc raising funds for charitable institution without an agreement in prescribed form

(1) It shall be unlawful for a professional fund-raiser to solicit money or other property for the benefit of a charitable institution unless he does so in accordance with an agreement with the institution satisfying the prescribed requirements.

(2) It shall be unlawful for a commercial participator to represent that charitable contributions are to be given to or applied for the benefit of a charitable institution

unless he does so in accordance with an agreement with the institution satisfying the prescribed requirements.

(3) Where on the application of a charitable institution the court is satisfied—

  (a) that any person has contravened or is contravening subsection (1) or (2) in relation to the institution, and

  (b) that, unless restrained, any such contravention is likely to continue or be repeated,

the court may grant an injunction restraining the contravention; and compliance with subsection (1) or (2) shall not be enforceable otherwise than in accordance with this subsection.

(4) Where—

  (a) a charitable institution makes any agreement with a professional fund-raiser or a commercial participator by virtue of which—

    (i) the professional fund-raiser is authorised to solicit money or other property for the benefit of the institution, or

    (ii) the commercial participator is authorised to represent that charitable contributions are to be given to or applied for the benefit of the institution,

    as the case may be, but

  (b) the agreement does not satisfy the prescribed requirements in any respect,

the agreement shall not be enforceable against the institution except to such extent (if any) as may be provided by an order of the court.

(5) A professional fund-raiser or commercial participator who is a party to such an agreement as is mentioned in subsection (4)(a) shall not be entitled to receive any amount by way of remuneration or expenses in respect of anything done by him in pursuance of the agreement unless—

  (a) he is so entitled under any provision of the agreement, and

  (b) either—

    (i) the agreement satisfies the prescribed requirements, or

    (ii) any such provision has effect by virtue of an order of the court under subsection (4).

(6) In this section "the prescribed requirements" means such requirements as are prescribed by regulations made by virtue of section 64(2)(a).

> **S.59** – *It is unlawful for a PFR to solicit money on behalf of a charitable institution unless he has previously entered into an agreement in the prescribed form. The same applies to the activity of a CP. The High Court has power to grant an injunction to stop contravention of this section.*

Use of an agreement in the prescribed form is important because, even if there is some other form of agreement in relation to the work of a PFR or CP, that agreement is not enforceable against the charitable institution without a Court Order.

S.59(5) – Emphasises that the PFR and the CP are not entitled to receive or keep money raised from the public by their activities unless:

- *the agreement says so and*

- *either the agreement is in the prescribed form or the Court has given its approval*

Note that it is the PFR or the CP who suffers from a failure to enter into the prescribed agreement and not the charitable institution itself. In practice however, it is suggested that the charitable institution would be well advised to enter into such an agreement because an argument with a PFR or CP can only serve to damage its reputation with business sponsors and the public generally.

60 Professional fund-raisers etc required to indicate institutions benefiting and arrangements for remuneration

(1) Where a professional fund-raiser solicits money or other property for the benefit of one or more particular charitable institutions, the solicitation shall be accompanied by a statement clearly indicating—

   (a) the name or names of the institution or institutions concerned;
   (b) if there is more than one institution concerned, the proportions in which the institutions are respectively to benefit; and
   (c) (in general terms) the method by which the fund-raiser's remuneration in connection with the appeal is to be determined.

(2) Where a professional fund-raiser solicits money or other property for charitable, benevolent or philanthropic purposes of any description (rather than for the benefit of one or more particular charitable institutions), the solicitation shall be accompanied by a statement clearly indicating—

   (a) the fact that he is soliciting money or other property for those purposes and not for the benefit of any particular charitable institution or institutions;
   (b) the method by which it is to be determined how the proceeds of the appeal are to be distributed between different charitable institutions; and
   (c) (in general terms) the method by which his remuneration in connection with the appeal is to be determined.

(3) Where any representation is made by a commercial participator to the effect that charitable contributions are to be given to or applied for the benefit of one or more particular charitable institutions, the representation shall be accompanied by a statement clearly indicating—

(a) the name or names of the institution or institutions concerned;

(b) if there is more than one institution concerned, the proportions in which the institutions are respectively to benefit; and

(c) (in general terms) the method by which it is to be determined—

    (i) what proportion of the consideration given for goods or services sold or supplied by him, or of any other proceeds of a promotional venture undertaken by him, is to be given to or applied for the benefit of the institution or institutions concerned, or

    (ii) what sums by way of donations by him in connection with the sale or supply of any such goods or services are to be so given or applied,

    as the case may require.

(4) If any such solicitation or representation as is mentioned in any of subsections (1) to (3) is made—

(a) in the course of a radio or television programme, and

(b) in association with an announcement to the effect that payment may be made, in response to the solicitation or representation, by means of a credit or debit card,

the statement required by virtue of subsection (1), (2) or (3) (as the case may be) shall include full details of the right to have refunded under section 61(1) any payment of £50 or more which is so made.

(5) If any such solicitation or representation as is mentioned in any of subsections (1) to (3) is made orally but is not made—

(a) by speaking directly to the particular person or persons to whom it is addressed and in his or their presence, or

(b) in the course of any radio or television programme,

the professional fund-raiser or commercial participator concerned shall, within seven days of any payment of £50 or more being made to him in response to the solicitation or representation, give to the person making the payment a written statement—

    (i) of the matters specified in paragraphs (a) to (c) of that subsection; and

    (ii) including full details of the right to cancel under section 61(2) an agreement made in response to the solicitation or representation, and the right to have refunded under section 61(2) or (3) any payment of £50 or more made in response thereto.

(6) In subsection (5) above the reference to the making of a payment is a reference to the making of a payment of whatever nature and by whatever means, including a payment made by means of a credit card or a debit card; and for the purposes of that subsection—

(a) where the person making any such payment makes it in person, it shall be regarded as made at the time when it is so made;

(b) where the person making any such payment sends it by post, it shall be regarded as made at the time when it is posted; and

(c) where the person making any such payment makes it by giving, by telephone or by means of any other telecommunication apparatus, authority for an account to be debited with the payment, it shall be regarded as made at the time when any such authority is given.

(7) Where any requirement of subsections (1) to (5) is not complied with in relation to any solicitation or representation, the professional fund-raiser or commercial participator concerned shall be guilty of an offence and liable on summary conviction to a fine not exceeding the fifth level on the standard scale.

(8) It shall be a defence for a person charged with any such offence to prove that he took all reasonable precautions and exercised all due diligence to avoid the commission of the offence.

(9) Where the commission by any person of an offence under subsection (7) is due to the act or default of some other person, that other person shall be guilty of the offence; and a person may be charged with and convicted of the offence by virtue of this subsection whether or not proceedings are taken against the first-mentioned person.

(10)   In this section—

"the appeal", in relation to any solicitation by a professional fund- raiser, means the campaign or other fund-raising venture in the course of which the solicitation is made;

"telecommunication apparatus" has the same meaning as in the Telecommunications Act 1984.

S.60 – *The PFR is required to make clear (though this does not have to be in writing) the name of the charitable institution(s) for which he is raising money and the proportions in which the money is being raised (if more than one), plus the method of his remuneration. The same applies if he is soliciting money for charitable benevolent or philanthropic purposes generally rather than for individual institutions.*

Statements by the CP also need to contain the same information as those by the PFR except that, instead of the method of remuneration, the CP has to indicate what proportion of the consideration given for goods and services will go to the charitable institution or how much has been paid by way of donations.

Any donor or customer who has responded to the invitations or representations of the PFR or the CP to the extent of £50 or more must be told of his right to ask for a refund after a 7 day cooling off period. Information about the cooling off period must be in writing unless the solicitation or representation is made in person or in a radio or television programme.

The PFR or the CP can be subject to criminal prosecution if he fails without taking reasonable precautions, to comply with this section.

61 Cancellation of payments and agreements made in response to appeals

(1) Where—

    (a) a person ("the donor"), in response to any such solicitation or representation as is mentioned in any of subsections (1) to (3) of section 60 which is made in the course of a radio or television programme, makes any payment of £50 or more to the relevant fund-raiser by means of a credit card or a debit card, but

    (b) before the end of the period of seven days beginning with the date of the solicitation or representation, the donor serves on the relevant fund-raiser a notice in writing which, however expressed, indicates the donor's intention to cancel the payment,

the donor shall (subject to subsection (4) below) be entitled to have the payment refunded to him forthwith by the relevant fund-raiser.

(2) Where—

    (a) a person ("the donor"), in response to any solicitation or representation falling within subsection (5) of section 60, enters into an agreement with the relevant fund-raiser under which the donor is, or may be, liable to make any payment or payments to the relevant fund-raiser, and the amount or aggregate amount which the donor is, or may be, liable to pay to him under the agreement is £50 or more, but

    (b) before the end of the period of seven days beginning with the date when he is given any such written statement as is referred to in that subsection, the donor serves on the relevant fund-raiser a notice in writing which, however expressed, indicates the donor's intention to cancel the agreement,

the notice shall operate, as from the time when it is so served, to cancel the agreement and any liability of any person other than the donor in connection with the making of any such payment or payments, and the donor shall (subject to subsection (4) below) be entitled to have any payment of £50 or more made by him under the agreement refunded to him forthwith by the relevant fund-raiser.

(3) Where, in response to any solicitation or representation falling within subsection (5) of section 60, a person ("the donor")—

    (a) makes any payment of £50 or more to the relevant fund-raiser, but

    (b) does not enter into any such agreement as is mentioned in subsection (2) above,

then, if before the end of the period of seven days beginning with the date when the donor is given any such written statement as is referred to in subsection (5) of that section, the donor serves on the relevant fund-raiser a notice in writing which, however expressed, indicates the donor's intention to cancel the payment, the donor shall (subject to subsection (4) below) be entitled to have the payment refunded to him forthwith by the relevant fund-raiser.

(4) The right of any person to have a payment refunded to him under any of subsections (1) to (3) above—

(a) is a right to have refunded to him the amount of the payment less any administrative expenses reasonably incurred by the relevant fund-raiser in connection with—
   (i) the making of the refund, or
   (ii) (in the case of a refund under subsection (2)) dealing with the notice of cancellation served by that person; and
(b) shall, in the case of a payment for goods already received, be conditional upon restitution being made by him of the goods in question.

(5) Nothing in subsections (1) to (3) above has effect in relation to any payment made or to be made in respect of services which have been supplied at the time when the relevant notice is served.

(6) In this section any reference to the making of a payment is a reference to the making of a payment of whatever nature and (in the case of subsection (2) or (3)) a payment made by whatever means, including a payment made by means of a credit card or a debit card; and subsection (6) of section 60 shall have effect for determining when a payment is made for the purposes of this section as it has effect for determining when a payment is made for the purposes of subsection (5) of that section.

(7) In this section "the relevant fund-raiser", in relation to any solicitation or representation, means the professional fund-raiser or commercial participator by whom it is made.

(8) The Secretary of State may by order—

(a) amend any provision of this section by substituting a different sum for the sum for the time being specified there; and
(b) make such consequential amendments in section 60 as he considers appropriate.

S.61 – *Provides for a cooling off period of 7 days during which a donor or customer can ask for a refund for any payment of £50 or more paid by credit or debit card and that includes an agreement to pay by instalments. Under S.61(4) the PFR or the CP can deduct reasonable administrative expenses but any right of the donor to a refund is on the basis that any goods received are returned.*

The section also applies to a situation where a donor enters into an agreement to pay £50 or more, whether or not by instalments.

This right to ask for a refund does not extend to payments for services actually supplied at the time.

The Home Secretary can by order amend the provisions in this section but there is no current intention to do so.

62 Right of charitable institution to prevent unauthorised fund-raising

(1) Where on the application of any charitable institution—

    (a) the court is satisfied that any person has done or is doing either of the following, namely—
        (i) soliciting money or other property for the benefit of the institution, or
        (ii) representing that charitable contributions are to be given to or applied for the benefit of the institution,

    and that, unless restrained, he is likely to do further acts of that nature, and

    (b) the court is also satisfied as to one or more of the matters specified in subsection (2),

then (subject to subsection (3)) the court may grant an injunction restraining the doing of any such acts.

(2) The matters referred to in subsection (1)(b) are—

    (a) that the person in question is using methods of fund-raising to which the institution objects;
    (b) that that person is not a fit and proper person to raise funds for the institution; and
    (c) where the conduct complained of is the making of such representations as are mentioned in subsection (1)(a)(ii), that the institution does not wish to be associated with the particular promotional or other fund-raising venture in which that person is engaged.

(3) The power to grant an injunction under subsection (1) shall not be exercisable on the application of a charitable institution unless the institution has, not less than 28 days before making the application, served on the person in question a notice in writing—

    (a) requesting him to cease forthwith—
        (i) soliciting money or other property for the benefit of the institution, or
        (ii) representing that charitable contributions are to be given to or applied for the benefit of the institution,

    as the case may be; and

    (b) stating that, if he does not comply with the notice, the institution will make an application under this section for an injunction.

(4) Where—

    (a) a charitable institution has served on any person a notice under subsection (3) ("the relevant notice") and that person has complied with the notice, but
    (b) that person has subsequently begun to carry on activities which are the same, or substantially the same, as those in respect of which the relevant notice was served,

the institution shall not, in connection with an application made by it under this section in respect of the activities carried on by that person, be required by virtue of that subsection to serve a further notice on him, if the application is made not more than 12 months after the date of service of the relevant notice.

(5) This section shall not have the effect of authorising a charitable institution to make an application under this section in respect of anything done by a professional fund-raiser or commercial participator in relation to the institution.

> **S.62** – *In circumstances where there is no PFR or CP, the Court can still intervene to prevent unauthorised fund raising if methods are objectionable, if the fund-raiser's credentials are wanting or if the charitable institution does not wish to be associated with it.*
>
> *However, the charitable institution has first to give the fund-raiser 28 days prior written notice and only then can the charitable institution ask for an injunction; although it can do so if the fund-raiser repeats his activities within 12 months.*
>
> *The Commission recommend the vetting of methods of unsolicited fund raisers. If a charity were to receive funds which it thought had been raised by improper methods, it could ask the Commission for a waiver under S.27 of the 1993 Act to allow it to refuse the donations, though the Commission would no doubt wish to take into account, and even make orders for, the destination of those funds if in fact the charity received the funds.*

63 False statements relating to institutions which are not registered charities

(1) Where—

    (a) a person solicits money or other property for the benefit of an institution in association with a representation that the institution is a registered charity, and

    (b) the institution is not such a charity,

he shall be guilty of an offence and liable on summary conviction to a fine not exceeding the fifth level on the standard scale.

[(1A) In any proceedings for an offence under subsection (1), it shall be a defence for the accused to prove that he believed on reasonable grounds that the institution was a registered charity.]

(2) In [this section] "registered charity" means a charity which is for the time being registered in the register of charities kept under [section 3 of the Charities Act 1993].

S.63 – *Provides that it is an offence in relation to fund raising to say that a charitable institution is a registered charity if it is not, unless the fund-raiser had reasonable grounds to think so. Given the ease with which the register of charities can be accessed via the internet, it might be thought that there is little excuse for getting this wrong.*

Supplementary

64 Regulations about fund-raising

(1) The Secretary of State may make such regulations as appear to him to be necessary or desirable for any purposes connected with any of the preceding provisions of this Part.

(2) Without prejudice to the generality of subsection (1), any such regulations may—

    (a) prescribe the form and content of—
        (i) agreements made for the purposes of section 59, and
        (ii) notices served under section 62(3);

    (b) require professional fund-raisers or commercial participators who are parties to such agreements with charitable institutions to make available to the institutions books, documents or other records (however kept) which relate to the institutions;

    (c) specify the manner in which money or other property acquired by professional fund-raisers or commercial participators for the benefit of, or otherwise falling to be given to or applied by such persons for the benefit of, charitable institutions is to be transmitted to such institutions;

    (d) provide for any provisions of section 60 or 61 having effect in relation to solicitations or representations made in the course of radio or television programmes to have effect, subject to any modifications specified in the regulations, in relation to solicitations or representations made in the course of such programmes—
        (i) by charitable institutions, or
        (ii) by companies connected with such institutions,

    and, in that connection, provide for any other provisions of this Part to have effect for the purposes of the regulations subject to any modifications so specified;

    (e) make other provision regulating the raising of funds for charitable, benevolent or philanthropic purposes (whether by professional fund-raisers or commercial participators or otherwise).

(3) In subsection (2)(c) the reference to such money or other property as is there mentioned includes a reference to money or other property which, in the case of a professional fund-raiser or commercial participator—

(a) has been acquired by him otherwise than in accordance with an agreement with a charitable institution, but

(b) by reason of any solicitation or representation in consequence of which it has been acquired, is held by him on trust for such an institution.

(4) Regulations under this section may provide that any failure to comply with a specified provision of the regulations shall be an offence punishable on summary conviction by a fine not exceeding the second level on the standard scale.

S.64 – *Provides power for the Home Secretary to make regulations under Part II of the Act and these have indeed been made – namely the Charitable Institutions (Fund Raising) Regulations 1994 (SI.3024) which reflect the guidelines in S.64(2) and which came into force on 1st March 1995.*

PART III

PUBLIC CHARITABLE COLLECTIONS

Part III: Public Charitable Collections: General Note
Although much of the 1992 and 1993 Acts have been in force for several years, the new, integrated provisions on public charitable collections, designed to replace existing and very old legislation on house to house and street collections, are not yet in force. Whether they ever will be without significant amendment is open to doubt given that there have already been wide consultations within the charity sector and amongst police forces and local authorities which have not resulted in either Part III being implemented or new legislation being introduced to replace Part III. It is not therefore considered that a commentary on Part III of the Act at this stage would be particularly helpful, though the text of Part III follows this note.

These brief guidelines, based on existing legislation and good practice may be helpful:-

Guidelines for Public Charitable Collections

1.   Street Collections
These are currently regulated by the Police, Factories, etc. (Miscellaneous Provisions) Act 1916.

Collecting money or selling goods for charity in streets or public places generally require a permit or licence:

- *in the City of London from the Common Council*

- *in the rest of London from the Metropolitan Police*

- *in the rest of England and Wales from the local authority.*

This would apply to carnivals, flag days or rag weeks.

2.   House to House Collections

These are currently regulated by the House-to-House Collections Act 1939 and by regulations made under that Act.

House to house collections (including visits to pubs and offices) also require similar licences to Street Collections, though permanent exemptions can be obtained from the Home Office for collections over a wide area and temporary exemptions can be obtained from the local police.

3.   Lotteries

These are regulated by the Lotteries and Amusements Act 1976:

- *Society Lotteries need to be registered with the Gaming Board (or if under £20,000 in ticket value, with the local authority)*

- *Small Lotteries do not need to be registered if incidental to fetes, bazaars, and other events, subject to certain conditions (for example no cash prizes).*

4.   Suggested Guidelines for Collection Organisers

- *Ensure that collectors know which charity they are collecting for; it is better for collectors to hand out leaflets than to try to explain to donors what the money will be used for, which might result in the charity being committed to spending the money on a restricted basis.*

- *Ensure that the charity knows when and where the collection is to take place and has given its permission.*

- *As cash is being handled, collectors should be over 18 or at least accompanied by an adult. This is for the security of the collectors as much as for protection of the money.*

- *Issue standard badges, sashes or tabards to collectors to include the charity's name.*

- *Each collector or group of collectors should also carry a written authority from the charity (which should comply with S.5 of the 1993 Act).*

- *Collecting tins should be numbered, sealed and opened only in the presence of people designated by the charity.*

- *Preferably collecting tins should have closed lids but where open buckets are used for collection (e.g. at a sporting event) these should be labelled, numbered and returned to a secure point for emptying as often as possible.*

- *Cash should be banked and a return made to the charity or its relevant branch as quickly as possible.*

5. Further Information

Further information about public charitable collections can be obtained from :

- *the Charity Commission's Guidance Notes CC20 and CC20(a) – see the Introduction*

- *the Institute of Charity Fundraising Managers, Central Office, Market Towers, 1 Nine Elms Lane, London SW8 5NQ. Tel: 0207 627 3436.*

65 Interpretation of Part III

Preliminary

(1) In this Part—

    (a) "public charitable collection" means (subject to subsection (2)) a charitable appeal which is made—
      (i) in any public place, or
      (ii) by means of visits from house to house; and
    (b) "charitable appeal" means an appeal to members of the public to give money or other property (whether for consideration or otherwise) which is made in association with a representation that the whole or any part of its proceeds is to be applied for charitable, benevolent or philanthropic purposes.

(2) Subsection (1)(a) does not apply to a charitable appeal which—

    (a) is made in the course of a public meeting; or
    (b) is made—
      (i) on land within a churchyard or burial ground contiguous or adjacent to a place of public worship, or
      (ii) on other land occupied for the purposes of a place of public worship and contiguous or adjacent to it,

    being (in each case) land which is enclosed or substantially enclosed (whether by any wall or building or otherwise); or

    (c) is an appeal to members of the public to give money or other property by placing it in an unattended receptacle;

and for the purposes of paragraph (c) above a receptacle is unattended if it is not in the possession or custody of a person acting as a collector.

(3) In this Part, in relation to a public charitable collection—

(a) "promoter" means a person who (whether alone or with others and whether for remuneration or otherwise) organises or controls the conduct of the charitable appeal in question, and associated expressions shall be construed accordingly; and

(b) "collector" means any person by whom that appeal is made (whether made by him alone or with others and whether made by him for remuneration or otherwise);

but where no person acts in the manner mentioned in paragraph (a) above in respect of a public charitable collection, any person who acts as a collector in respect of it shall for the purposes of this Part be treated as a promoter of it as well.

(4) In this Part—

"local authority" means the council of a [Welsh county or county borough, of a] district or of a London borough, the Common Council of the City of London, or the Council of the Isles of Scilly; and

"proceeds", in relation to a public charitable collection, means all money or other property given (whether for consideration or otherwise) in response to the charitable appeal in question.

(5) In this Part any reference to charitable purposes, where occurring in the context of a reference to charitable, benevolent or philanthropic purposes, is a reference to charitable purposes whether or not the purposes are charitable within the meaning of any rule of law.

(6) The functions exercisable under this Part by a local authority shall be exercisable—

(a) as respects the Inner Temple, by its Sub-Treasurer, and

(b) as respects the Middle Temple, by its Under Treasurer;

and references in this Part to a local authority or to the area of a local authority shall be construed accordingly.

(7) It is hereby declared that an appeal to members of the public (other than one falling within subsection (2)) is a public charitable collection for the purposes of this Part if—

(a) it consists in or includes the making of an offer to sell goods or to supply services, or the exposing of goods for sale, to members of the public, and

(b) it is made as mentioned in sub-paragraph (i) or (ii) of subsection (1)(a) and in association with a representation that the whole or any part of its proceeds is to be applied for charitable, benevolent or philanthropic purposes.

This subsection shall not be taken as prejudicing the generality of subsection (1)(b).

(8) In this section—

"house" includes any part of a building constituting a separate dwelling;

"public place", in relation to a charitable appeal, means—

(a) any highway, and
(b) (subject to subsection (9)) any other place to which, at any time when the appeal is made, members of the public have or are permitted to have access and which either—
    (i) is not within a building, or
    (ii) if within a building, is a public area within any station, airport or shopping precinct or any other similar public area.

(9) In subsection (8), paragraph (b) of the definition of "public place" does not apply to—

(a) any place to which members of the public are permitted to have access only if any payment or ticket required as a condition of access has been made or purchased; or
(b) any place to which members of the public are permitted to have access only by virtue of permission given for the purposes of the appeal in question.

Prohibition on conducting unauthorised collections

66 Prohibition on conducting public charitable collections without authorisation

(1) No public charitable collection shall be conducted in the area of any local authority except in accordance with—

(a) a permit issued by the authority under section 68; or
(b) an order made by the Charity Commissioners under section 72.

(2) Where a public charitable collection is conducted in contravention of subsection (1), any promoter of that collection shall be guilty of an offence and liable on summary conviction to a fine not exceeding the fourth level on the standard scale.

Permits

67 Applications for permits to conduct public charitable collections

(1) An application for a permit to conduct a public charitable collection in the area of a local authority shall be made to the authority by the person or persons proposing to promote that collection.

(2) Any such application—

(a) shall specify the period for which it is desired that the permit, if issued, should have effect, being a period not exceeding 12 months; and

(b) shall contain such information as may be prescribed by regulations under section 73.

(3) Any such application—

(a) shall be made at least one month before the relevant day or before such later date as the local authority may in the case of that application allow, . . .

(b) . . .

and for this purpose "the relevant day" means the day on which the collection is to be conducted or, where it is to be conducted on more than one day, the first of those days.

(4) Before determining any application duly made to them under this section, a local authority shall consult the chief officer of police for the police area which comprises or includes their area and may make such other inquiries as they think fit.

68 Determination of applications and issue of permits

(1) Where an application for a permit is duly made to a local authority under section 67 in respect of a public charitable collection, the authority shall either—

(a) issue a permit in respect of the collection, or

(b) refuse the application on one or more of the grounds specified in section 69,

and, where they issue such a permit, it shall (subject to section 70) have effect for the period specified in the application in accordance with section 67(2)(a).

(2) A local authority may, at the time of issuing a permit under this section, attach to it such conditions as they think fit, having regard to the local circumstances of the collection; but the authority shall secure that the terms of any such conditions are consistent with the provisions of any regulations under section 73.

(3) Without prejudice to the generality of subsection (2), a local authority may attach conditions—

(a) specifying the day of the week, date, time or frequency of the collection;

(b) specifying the locality or localities within their area in which the collection may be conducted;

(c) regulating the manner in which the collection is to be conducted.

(4) Where a local authority—

(a) refuse to issue a permit, or

(b) attach any condition to a permit under subsection (2),

they shall serve on the applicant written notice of their decision to do so and of the reasons for their decision; and that notice shall also state the right of appeal conferred by section 71(1) or (as the case may be) section 71(2), and the time within which such an appeal must be brought.

69 Refusal of permits

(1) A local authority may refuse to issue a permit to conduct a public charitable collection on any of the following grounds, namely—

(a) that it appears to them that the collection would cause undue inconvenience to members of the public by reason of—
(i) the day of the week or date on which,
(ii) the time at which,
(iii) the frequency with which, or
(iv) the locality or localities in which,

it is proposed to be conducted;

(b) that the collection is proposed to be conducted on a day on which another public charitable collection is already authorised (whether under section 68 or otherwise) to be conducted in the authority's area, or on the day falling immediately before, or immediately after, any such day;

(c) that it appears to them that the amount likely to be applied for charitable, benevolent or philanthropic purposes in consequence of the collection would be inadequate, having regard to the likely amount of the proceeds of the collection;

(d) that it appears to them that the applicant or any other person would be likely to receive an excessive amount by way of remuneration in connection with the collection;

(e) that the applicant has been convicted—
(i) of an offence under section 5 of the 1916 Act, under the 1939 Act, under section 119 of the 1982 Act or regulations made under it, or under this Part or regulations made under section 73 below, or
(ii) of any offence involving dishonesty or of a kind the commission of which would in their opinion be likely to be facilitated by the issuing to him of a permit under section 68 above;

(f) where the applicant is a person other than a charitable, benevolent or philanthropic institution for whose benefit the collection is proposed to be conducted, that they are not satisfied that the applicant is authorised (whether by any such institution or by any person acting on behalf of any such institution) to promote the collection; or

(g) that it appears to them that the applicant, in promoting any other collection authorised under this Part or under section 119 of the 1982 Act, failed to exercise due diligence—
(i) to secure that persons authorised by him to act as collectors for the purposes of the collection were fit and proper persons;
(ii) to secure that such persons complied with the provisions of regulations under section 73 below or (as the case may be) section 119 of the 1982 Act; or
(iii) to prevent badges or certificates of authority being obtained by persons other than those he had so authorised.

(2) A local authority shall not, however, refuse to issue such a permit on the ground mentioned in subsection (1)(b) if it appears to them—

  (a) that the collection would be conducted only in one location, which is on land to which members of the public would have access only by virtue of the express or implied permission of the occupier of the land; and

  (b) that the occupier of the land consents to the collection being conducted there;

and for this purpose "the occupier", in relation to unoccupied land, means the person entitled to occupy it.

(3) In subsection (1)—

  (a) in the case of a collection in relation to which there is more than one applicant, any reference to the applicant shall be construed as a reference to any of the applicants; and

  (b) (subject to subsection (4)) the reference in paragraph (g)(iii) to badges or certificates of authority is a reference to badges or certificates of authority in a form prescribed by regulations under section 73 below or (as the case may be) under section 119 of the 1982 Act.

(4) Subsection (1)(g) applies to the conduct of the applicant (or any of the applicants) in relation to any public charitable collection authorised under regulations made under section 5 of the 1916 Act (collection of money or sale of articles in a street or other public place), or authorised under the 1939 Act (collection of money or other property by means of visits from house to house), as it applies to his conduct in relation to a collection authorised under this Part, subject to the following modifications, namely—

  (a) in the case of a collection authorised under regulations made under the 1916 Act—

    (i) the reference in sub-paragraph (ii) to regulations under section 73 below shall be construed as a reference to the regulations under which the collection in question was authorised, and

    (ii) the reference in sub-paragraph (iii) to badges or certificates of authority shall be construed as a reference to any written authority provided to a collector pursuant to those regulations; and

  (b) in the case of a collection authorised under the 1939 Act—

    (i) the reference in sub-paragraph (ii) to regulations under section 73 below shall be construed as a reference to regulations under section 4 of that Act, and

    (ii) the reference in sub-paragraph (iii) to badges or certificates of authority shall be construed as a reference to badges or certificates of authority in a form prescribed by such regulations.

(5) In this section—

"the 1916 Act" means the Police, Factories, &c (Miscellaneous Provisions) Act 1916;

"the 1939 Act" means the House to House Collections Act 1939; and

"the 1982 Act" means the Civic Government (Scotland) Act 1982.

70 Withdrawal etc of permits

(1) Where a local authority who have issued a permit under section 68—

(a) have reason to believe that there has been a change in the circumstances which prevailed at the time when they issued the permit, and are of the opinion that, if the application for the permit had been made in the new circumstances of the case, the permit would not have been issued by them, or

(b) have reason to believe that any information furnished to them by the promoter (or, in the case of a collection in relation to which there is more than one promoter, by any of them) for the purposes of the application for the permit was false in a material particular,

then (subject to subsection (2)) they may—

(i) withdraw the permit;
(ii) attach any condition to the permit; or
(iii) vary any existing condition of the permit.

(2) Any condition imposed by the local authority under subsection (1) (whether by attaching a new condition to the permit or by varying an existing condition) must be one that could have been attached to the permit under section 68(2) at the time when it was issued, assuming for this purpose—

(a) that the new circumstances of the case had prevailed at that time, or

(b) (in a case falling within paragraph (b) of subsection (1) above) that the authority had been aware of the true circumstances of the case at that time.

(3) Where a local authority who have issued a permit under section 68 have reason to believe that there has been or is likely to be a breach of any condition of it, or that a breach of such a condition is continuing, they may withdraw the permit.

(4) Where under this section a local authority withdraw, attach any condition to, or vary an existing condition of, a permit, they shall serve on the promoter written notice of their decision to do so and of the reasons for their decision; and that notice shall also state the right of appeal conferred by section 71(2) and the time within which such an appeal must be brought.

(5) Where a local authority so withdraw, attach any condition to, or vary an existing condition of, a permit, the permit shall nevertheless continue to have effect as if it had not been withdrawn or (as the case may be) as if the condition had not been attached or the variation had not been made—

(a) until the time for bringing an appeal under section 71(2) has expired, or

(b) if such an appeal is duly brought, until the determination or abandonment of the appeal.

71 Appeals

(1) A person who has duly applied to a local authority under section 67 for a permit to conduct a public charitable collection in the authority's area may appeal to a magistrates' court against a decision of the authority to refuse to issue a permit to him.

(2) A person to whom a permit has been issued under section 68 may appeal to a magistrates' court against—

(a) a decision of the local authority under that section or section 70 to attach any condition to the permit; or

(b) a decision of the local authority under section 70 to vary any condition so attached or to withdraw the permit.

(3) An appeal under subsection (1) or (2) shall be by way of complaint for an order, and the Magistrates' Courts Act 1980 shall apply to the proceedings; and references in this section to a magistrates' court are to a magistrates' court acting for the petty sessions area in which is situated the office or principal office of the local authority against whose decision the appeal is brought.

(4) Any such appeal shall be brought within 14 days of the date of service on the person in question of the relevant notice under section 68(4) or (as the case may be) section 70(4); and for the purposes of this subsection an appeal shall be taken to be brought when the complaint is made.

(5) An appeal against the decision of a magistrates' court on an appeal under subsection (1) or (2) may be brought to the Crown Court.

(6) On an appeal to a magistrates' court or the Crown Court under this section, the court may confirm, vary or reverse the local authority's decision and generally give such directions as it thinks fit, having regard to the provisions of this Part and of regulations under section 73.

(7) It shall be the duty of the local authority to comply with any directions given by the court under subsection (6); but the authority need not comply with any directions given by a magistrates' court—

(a) until the time for bringing an appeal under subsection (5) has expired, or

(b) if such an appeal is duly brought, until the determination or abandonment of the appeal.

Orders made by Charity Commissioners

72 Orders made by Charity Commissioners

(1) Where the Charity Commissioners are satisfied, on the application of any charity, that that charity proposes—

(a) to promote public charitable collections—

    (i) throughout England and Wales, or

    (ii) throughout a substantial part of England and Wales,

  in connection with any charitable purposes pursued by the charity, or

(b) to authorise other persons to promote public charitable collections as mentioned in paragraph (a),

the Commissioners may make an order under this subsection in respect of the charity.

(2) Such an order shall have the effect of authorising public charitable collections which—

  (a) are promoted by the charity in respect of which the order is made, or by persons authorised by the charity, and

  (b) are so promoted in connection with the charitable purposes mentioned in subsection (1),

to be conducted in such area or areas as may be specified in the order.

(3) An order under subsection (1) may—

  (a) include such conditions as the Commissioners think fit;

  (b) be expressed (without prejudice to paragraph (c)) to have effect without limit of time, or for a specified period only;

  (c) be revoked or varied by a further order of the Commissioners.

(4) Where the Commissioners, having made an order under subsection (1) in respect of a charity, make any further order revoking or varying that order, they shall serve on the charity written notice of their reasons for making the further order, unless it appears to them that the interests of the charity would not be prejudiced by the further order.

[(5) Section 89(1), (2) and (4) of the Charities Act 1993 (provisions as to orders made by the Commissioners) shall apply to an order made by them under this section as it applies to an order made by them under that Act.

(6) In this section "charity" and "charitable purposes" have the same meaning as in that Act.]

Supplementary

73 Regulations

(1) The Secretary of State may make regulations—

  (a) prescribing the information which is to be contained in applications made under section 67;

  (b) for the purpose of regulating the conduct of public charitable collections authorised under—

    (i) permits issued under section 68; or

(ii) orders made by the Charity Commissioners under section 72.

(2) Regulations under subsection (1)(b) may, without prejudice to the generality of that provision, make provision—

(a) about the keeping and publication of accounts;

(b) for the prevention of annoyance to members of the public;

(c) with respect to the use by collectors of badges and certificates of authority, or badges incorporating such certificates, and to other matters relating to such badges and certificates, including, in particular, provision—

  (i) prescribing the form of such badges and certificates;

  (ii) requiring a collector, on request, to permit his badge, or any certificate of authority held by him for the purposes of the collection, to be inspected by a constable or a duly authorised officer of a local authority, or by an occupier of any premises visited by him in the course of the collection;

(d) for prohibiting persons under a prescribed age from acting as collectors, and prohibiting others from causing them so to act.

(3) Regulations under this section may provide that any failure to comply with a specified provision of the regulations shall be an offence punishable on summary conviction by a fine not exceeding the second level on the standard scale.

74 Offences

(1) A person shall be guilty of an offence if, in connection with any charitable appeal, he displays or uses—

(a) a prescribed badge or a prescribed certificate of authority which is not for the time being held by him for the purposes of the appeal pursuant to regulations under section 73, or

(b) any badge or article, or any certificate or other document, so nearly resembling a prescribed badge or (as the case may be) a prescribed certificate of authority as to be likely to deceive a member of the public.

(2) A person guilty of an offence under subsection (1) shall be liable on summary conviction to a fine not exceeding the fourth level on the standard scale.

(3) Any person who, for the purposes of an application made under section 67, knowingly or recklessly furnishes any information which is false in a material particular shall be guilty of an offence and liable on summary conviction to a fine not exceeding the fourth level on the standard scale.

[(3A) Any person who knowingly or recklessly provides the Commissioners with information which is false or misleading in a material particular shall be guilty of an offence if the information is provided in circumstances in which he intends, or could reasonably be expected to know, that it would be used by them for the purpose of discharging their functions under section 72.

(3B) A person guilty of an offence under subsection (3A) shall be liable—

(a) on summary conviction, to a fine not exceeding the statutory maximum;

(b) on conviction or indictment, to imprisonment for a term not exceeding two years or to a fine, or both.]

(4) In subsection (1) "prescribed badge" and "prescribed certificate of authority" mean respectively a badge and a certificate of authority in such form as may be prescribed by regulations under section 73.

S.65 to S.74 *For reasons set out in the General Note above there is no commentary on Part III of the Act.*

PART IV

GENERAL

75 Offences by bodies corporate

Where any offence—

(a) under this Act or any regulations made under it, or

(b) . . .

is committed by a body corporate and is proved to have been committed with the consent or connivance of, or to be attributable to any neglect on the part of, any director, manager, secretary or other similar officer of the body corporate, or any person who was purporting to act in any such capacity, he as well as the body corporate shall be guilty of that offence and shall be liable to be proceeded against and punished accordingly.

In relation to a body corporate whose affairs are managed by its members, "director" means a member of the body corporate.

S.75 – *Provides that where an offence is committed by a corporate body, appropriate officers of the corporate body can also be prosecuted. There is a similar provision in S.95 of the 1993 Act.*

76 Service of documents

(1) This section applies to—

(a) . . .

(b) any notice or other document required or authorised to be given or served under Part II of this Act; and

(c) any notice required to be served under Part III of this Act.

(2) A document to which this section applies may be served on or given to a person (other than a body corporate)—

    (a) by delivering it to that person;
    (b) by leaving it at his last known address in the United Kingdom; or
    (c) by sending it by post to him at that address.

(3) A document to which this section applies may be served on or given to a body corporate by delivering it or sending it by post—

    (a) to the registered or principal office of the body in the United Kingdom, or
    (b) if it has no such office in the United Kingdom, to any place in the United Kingdom where it carries on business or conducts its activities (as the case may be).

(4) Any such document may also be served on or given to a person (including a body corporate) by sending it by post to that person at an address notified by that person for the purposes of this subsection to the person or persons by whom it is required or authorised to be served or given.

> **S.76** – *Provides for the service of documents or notices which are required to be served under Parts II or III of the Act.*

77 Regulations and orders

(1) Any regulations or order of the Secretary of State under this Act—

    (a) shall be made by statutory instrument; and
    (b) (subject to subsection (2)) shall be subject to annulment in pursuance of a resolution of either House of Parliament.

(2) Subsection (1)(b) does not apply—

    (a)–(c) . . . ; or
    (d) to an order under section 79(2).

(3) Any regulations or order of the Secretary of State under this Act may make—

    (a) different provision for different cases; and
    (b) such supplemental, incidental, consequential or transitional provision or savings as the Secretary of State considers appropriate.

(4) Before making any regulations under section . . . 64 or 73 the Secretary of State shall consult such persons or bodies of persons as he considers appropriate.

S.77 – *Provides for the Home Secretary to make regulations under the Act, as to which see S.64 above.*

78 Minor and consequential amendments and repeals

(1) The enactments mentioned in Schedule 6 to this Act shall have effect subject to the amendments there specified (which are either minor amendments or amendments consequential on the provisions of this Act).

(2) The enactments mentioned in Schedule 7 to this Act (which include some that are already spent or are no longer of practical utility) are hereby repealed to the extent specified in the third column of that Schedule.

S.78 – *Provides for the minor amendments set out in Schedule 6 and the repeals set out in Schedule 7.*

79 Short title, commencement and extent

(1) This Act may be cited as the Charities Act 1992.

(2) This Act shall come into force on such day as the Secretary of State may by order appoint; and different days may be so appointed for different provisions or for different purposes.

(3) Subject to subsections (4) to (6) below, this Act extends only to England and Wales.

(4), (5) . . .

(6) The amendments in Schedule 6, and (subject to subsection (7)) the repeals in Schedule 7, have the same extent as the enactments to which they refer, and section 78 extends accordingly.

(7) The repeal in Schedule 7 of the Police, Factories, &c (Miscellaneous Provisions) Act 1916 does not extend to Northern Ireland.

S.79 – *Confirms that, apart from specific instances, the Act applies only to England and Wales.*

SCHEDULE 7
REPEALS

Section 78(2)

Chapter	Short title	Extent of repeal
1872 c.24.	Charitable Trustees Incorporation Act 1872.	In section 2, the words from "and all" onwards. In section 4, the words from "; and the appointment" onwards. In section 5, the words from "; and nothing" onwards. In section 7, the words from "; and there" onwards. The Schedule.
1916 c.31.	Police, Factories, &c. (Miscellaneous Provisions) Act 1916.	The whole Act.
1939 c.44.	House to House Collections Act 1939.	The whole Act.
1940 c.31.	War Charities Act 1940.	The whole Act.
1948 c.29.	National Assistance Act 1948.	Section 41.
1958 c.49.	Trading Representations (Disabled Persons) Act 1958.	Section 1(2)(b).
1959 c.72.	Mental Health Act 1959.	Section 8(3).
1960 c.58.	Charities Act 1960.	In section 4(6), the words from "and any person" onwards. Section 6(6) and (9). Section 7(4). . . . Section 16(2). In section 19(6), the words "or the like reference from the Secretary of State". In section 22, subsection (6) and, in subsection (9), the words from ", and the" to "endowment" (where last occurring).

Chapter	Short title	Extent of repeal
		Section 27.
		Section 29.
		In section 30C(1)(c), the words "by or".
		Section 31.
		Section 44.
		In section 45(3), the words "Subject to subsection (9) of section twenty-two of this Act,".
		In section 46, the words ", subject to subsection (9) of section twenty-two of this Act,".
		In Schedule 1, in paragraph 1(3), the words "Subject to sub-paragraph (6) below,".
		In Schedule 6, the entry relating to the War Charities Act 1940.
1966 c.42.	Local Government Act 1966.	In Schedule 3, in column 1 of Part II, paragraph 20.
1968 c.60.	Theft Act 1968.	In Schedule 2, in Part III, the entry relating to the House to House Collections Act 1939.
1970 c.42.	Local Authority Social Services Act 1970.	In Schedule 1, the entry relating to section 41 of the National Assistance Act 1948.
1972 c.70.	Local Government Act 1972.	Section 210(8).
		In Schedule 29, paragraphs 22 and 23.
1983 c.41.	Health and Social Services and Social Security Adjudications Act 1983.	Section 30(3).
1983 c.47.	National Heritage Act 1983.	In Schedule 4, paragraphs 13 and 14.
1985 c.9.	Companies Consolidation (Consequential Provisions) Act 1985.	In Schedule 2, the entry relating to section 30(1) of the Charities Act 1960.

Chapter	Short title	Extent of repeal
. . .	. . .	. . .
1986 c.41.	Finance Act 1986.	Section 33.

Schedule 7 is no longer of any practical interest.

Index